# FAVOURITE AUSTRALIAN BIRDS

## Compiled by Louise Egerton

Writers: David Butcher; Andrew Detre; Gwen Jacobsen;
Greg Keith; Peter McDonald; Chris Mobbs; Penny and Gerry
Olsen; Ruth Smith; Mary-Jo Wilson.

BAY BOOKS

The Publisher wishes to thank Walter Boles, ornithologist, Australian Museum for his assistance during the production of this book.

## A Bay Books Publication

Bay Books, an imprint of
HarperCollins*Publishers*
25 Ryde Road, Pymble, Sydney, NSW 2073, Australia
31 View Road, Glenfield, Auckland 10, New Zealand

First published by Bay Books in 1988
This edition 1993

Copyright © Bay Books

National Library of Australia card number and
ISBN 1 86256 037 4

Typeset by Savage Type Pty Ltd, Brisbane
Printed in Singapore

9 8 7 6 5 4 3 2 1
96  95  94  93

# CONTENTS

| | |
|---|---|
| Wrens and Robins | 6 |
| Long-legged Fishermen | 14 |
| Birds of Prey | 25 |
| Parrot Parade | 34 |
| The Moundbuilders | 46 |
| The Webbed-feet Brigade | 52 |
| The Forest Dwellers | 64 |
| Birds of the High Seas | 76 |
| Flappers and Flippers | 87 |
| The Kingfisher Clan | 95 |
| Seasonal Visitors | 100 |
| Sounds of the Bush | 107 |
| Fascinating Finches | 116 |
| Birds of the Night | 122 |

# INTRODUCTION

Australia has some of the most distinctive and curious birds in the world. *Favourite Australian Birds*, filled with beautiful colour photographs, dips into this world. It tells you where to find them and what kind of habits to expect.

One thing most birds do better than any other living creatures is fly but here in Australia some species cannot fly at all. The grounded emu is far too heavy and has developed its legs rather than its wings. Others with considerable body weight and long legs are also reluctant fliers. For the bustard flying is a reluctant affair undertaken only as a last resort.

However not all heavy birds are poor fliers. The wandering albatross, which usually has to fling itself off a clifftop in order to fly, glides gracefully on the air currents once it is airborne and the ungainly-looking pelican is also something of a surprise. It is most impressive when fishing: its precision dive bombings providing an aeronautical display few could match.

The diversity of Australia's birds is a reflection of its many habitats. From the wetlands of the Northern Territory, where the long-legged jabirus stalk and the brolgas dance, to the heavily-wooded forests east of the Great Divide where frogmouths lurk unseen and lyrebirds scratch through the undergrowth, the whole continent vibrates with birdlife. Even in the centre, where the land is dusty and dry, flocks of budgerigars squeak and chatter on their way to the billabong as wedge-tailed eagles soar high above the low-scrub plains searching out their next meal.

Some of the most spectacular birds live in the tropical rainforests of northern Queensland. It is here that you will find the rare palm cockatoo, the bizarre cassowary and the magnificent paradise riflebird. In these cathedrals of towering hardwoods, birds are more frequently heard than seen.

Many Australian birds are well-known by their call. The whipbird, for example, in the more southerly forests of the eastern seaboard, is a common sound. The inescapable laughter of the kookaburra, the rollicking tunes of the currawongs, the high-pitched pipping tones of the bellbird and the noisy squawks of the sulphur-crested cockatoos are all sounds that are synonymous with the Australian bush.

The range of birds' behaviour is enormous. Some, like the bowerbirds, will go to great lengths to attract a mate, while for others courtship is a simple procedure. Feeding techniques vary too. Some birds, like the little pittas, have learnt to use tools while the frigatebird prefers to use bullying tactics. Some are fastidious nest builders. Others are sloppy.

*Favourite Australian Birds* can only be the beginning for armchair birdwatching enthusiasts. When you take a glimpse into the life of birds you quickly realise that there is still so much more to learn and know about our feathered friends.

# WRENS AND ROBINS

*Of Australia's small birds, the wren and robin families are surely the most colourful and endearing. Although some species of both of these groups are easily spotted in suburban gardens, others have penetrated the remote and dry interior of the continent.*

## Wrens

Australia's wrens are not closely related to those of the northern hemisphere or to those of New Zealand, but similar traits have given rise to the use of a common name. The wrens of Australia, known as fairy wrens, belong to the family Maluridae. There are five genera in the family, three of which have representatives in dry country: true fairy wrens *Malurus*, emu wrens *Stipiturus* and grasswrens *Amytornis*. The birds known as scrub wrens belong to the genus *Sericornis*, family Acanthizidae, and are restricted to mainly coastal, humid scrub and rainforest in eastern Australia.

Like all wrens, fairy wrens are perching songbirds, passerines. They live in the same patch of undergrowth all year, never travelling far, and glean and fossick for insects, some species eating seeds as well. Ground foragers among the true fairy wrens have thin, probe-like bills while several of the grasswrens in central Australia have evolved thick, finch-like bills to cope with the high proportion of seeds in their diet. The development of their rictal ('mouth') bristles or 'whiskers' is also highly variable according to the feeding habits of the species. These bristles protect the eyes and face when foraging.

Wrens' wings are rounded and ill-suited to prolonged flight, but as these birds run and hop a lot, their feet and legs are strong. The flight of true fairy wrens is a jerky flutter, of value only in flitting between feeding grounds or as a means of quick escape. The tail droops and is useless as a rudder. Grasswrens also flap laboriously with their tail dragging on the rare occasions when they do fly, just clearing the shrubs and travelling only about 50 metres. They are such

F. Park/A.N.T. Photo Library

strong, fast runners, bounding power-fully over rocks and racing across flats, that they rarely resort to flight. Emu wrens have almost dispensed with flight altogether and run along through the undergrowth with their filmy tails held straight behind them to avoid abrasion by the dense under-growth from which they seldom emerge — thus being seldom seen.

Wrens have evolved a rich vocal repertoire to defend their home territories and are usually heard before they are seen. Their habit of cocking their tails high over their backs is also an identity signal, being twitched vari-ously to signal intentions, like a flag signal code. This behaviour and a complex system of chirrups and churrs keeps wrens in constant contact with one another throughout their daily routines. Highly social birds, wrens roost, feed and breed communally and huddle together for mutual preening

sessions during the day between feed-ing sessions. The roosts where they cluster tightly to sleep are under thickets or on low sheltered branches.

Singing is primarily a male activity, though duets between mates are per-formed occasionally. During breeding, males engage in constant song battles with their neighbours, preferring to perform from perches with vantage points from which their voices carry well. While attack and defence dis-plays are elaborately exaggerated, sex-ual displays are so inconspicuous, so similar to daily routine activity such as huddling and preening, that they have not been identified, and copulation is quite perfunctory, taking place any-where without noticeable prelimi-naries.

Despite their many similarities, the various types of fairy wrens are also unique in many ways. One of the most notable features in the life of true fairy wrens is their family cohesion. A single female is mated to the dominant male

*OPPOSITE: The tiny emu wren with its emu-like tail feathers tends to pair off and breed at an early age.*
*LEFT: This purple-backed wren, which may have a nest of hungry chicks waiting, lives in different habitats ranging from dense vegetation to arid saltbush regions.*
*ABOVE: Cocking its tail high over its back is the blue wren's identity signal code. The blue wren has a number of different signals.*

in a group of up to a dozen birds. Though these groups were once thought to be 'harems' of females, almost the opposite is true. They are nearly all males in immature or non-breeding plumage, very much like that of the female. Most of these are offspring of the dominant pair. They remain with the parents for long periods of time, sometimes years, assisting in the rearing of the young, freeing the female to raise more broods, and assisting the dominant male in defence of the territory. Most young females are driven away either to mate and breed elsewhere or to perish. This protects against in-breeding as does the occasional chance recruitment of non-related males into the group.

Grasswrens and emu wrens tend to be more communally tolerant of females, and the offspring help less. Whereas true fairy wrens tend to be more inclined to produce in large numbers and so can lose individuals without affecting the whole, grasswrens tend to adopt a more miserly approach, each pair usually raising only one brood a year and tending them for months to make certain every one of them survives. In the emu wrens also, pairs breed individually then live and forage together in small family groups. Young emu wrens leave the family group after the first year and breed at an early age.

All fairy wrens weave dome-roofed nests of vegetable fibre, often with a bit of spider web for binding, and place them in low shrubs. Two to five eggs are laid on consecutive mornings and incubation is not begun until the clutch is complete so that all the eggs hatch together and the young fledge simultaneously. Females build alone — a new nest for each brood — and incubate alone. Hatchlings are naked and helpless and take between nine and thirteen days to acquire fluffy brown down. They are then herded out of the nest and off to cover where they are fed and defended while their strength and their long tails grow. To grow a long tail in a crowded, closed nest would be awkward if not impossible and evasion of predators is easier out of the nest.

Though the wrens of well-watered habitats are renowned for the bright blue nuptial plumage of the breeding males, species inhabiting barren plains and pale tussocky grasses adopt mostly dull brown and streaked camouflage

R. & D. Keller/A.N.T. Photo Library

plumage. The shaggy brown and russet white-streaked feathers of the grasswrens are a superb example of cryptic colouration, and the shagginess of the plumage protects it from abrasion by the stiff undergrowth in which the birds live. Emu wrens are tiny and dun coloured and have filmy, emu-like tail feathers. Although most of the fairy wren species in dry country are dull by comparison with their wet country cousins, some of the brightest fairy wrens are dry country birds.

Wrens moult once or twice a year, some changing their colouration and others retaining the same cryptic plumage throughout the year.

Various wren species living in close proximity to one another generally have somewhat different feeding preferences and habits. True fairy

*ABOVE: Although the yellow throated scrub wren is noted for its melodious singing, this tends to primarily be a male activity.*

wrens work from the ground to low trees in more open spaces while grasswrens forage mainly on the ground under cover of tussock and scrub. Emu wrens glean dense low thickets of undergrowth, up to about a metre above the ground. Various wren species have also evolved different plumage patterns and different songs. Studies have shown that although they are aware of each other's presence, the different species don't consider each other threats or rivals.

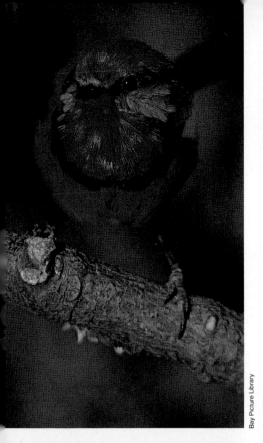

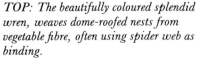

TOP: *The beautifully coloured splendid wren, weaves dome-roofed nests from vegetable fibre, often using spider web as binding.*
ABOVE: *A male red-backed wren feasts on a caterpillar catch.*
TOP RIGHT: *Mealtime for this blue wren chick. Both parents plus helpers feed the young.*

The natural predators of fairy wrens are goannas, snakes, butcher-birds and raptors, but even these are seldom successful as the wrens have acute hearing and have usually sounded alarm calls long before a predator has actually arrived. They also have a distraction display to lure predators away from occupied nests. This display is called the 'rodent run' as it resembles the scurrying of a mouse. It is thought to be a feigning of juvenile helplessness.

The greatest threat to wrens comes, of course, from man and his intro-duced animals. The clearing of the wrens' natural habitat for crops, pas-tures, forestry, mining or tax con-cessions is the most devastating. Both domestic and feral stock, such as cattle, sheep, donkeys, goats, pigs and rabbits trample and graze the natural

cover where the wrens live. Introduced predators such as foxes and feral cats take a much greater toll than natural predators, indeed, cats are the most efficient killers ever turned loose in Australia apart from their patron — man. Fires deliberately set to generate tender new growth for grazing are also devastating in their effect on wrens both because the tiny birds, hardly capable of flight, have little chance of escape unless they can find refuge in holes or deep rock crevices, and because even those that are not roasted alive have little chance of survival as several years may be required for their habitat to regenerate.

Few of these problems are recog-nised but the rarer wrens in the remote arid habitats of Australia seem far safer than those living in areas desir-able to humans.

9

# Robins

Nowadays, Australian robins belong to the *Eopsaltriidae* family. Contrary to popular myth, they do not belong to the family *Muscicapidae* which includes thrushes and blackbirds. Females tend to be more plainly dressed than males, to provide camouflage while on the nest.

This gender differentiation is true of one genus of robins; in two others the sexes are very similar in appearance; in another genus one species is similar, another distinct (*Drymodes*).

Muscicapidae means flycatchers — birds which catch insects on the wing. This is far from the robins' greatest skill. These birds are all insectivorous but most seem to feed by dropping from perch to ground, or by moving along the ground. Some also feed by exploring the bark of trees and the undersides of leaves.

They are small birds, 11–15 centimetres long, except for the scrub robins, which are 22–23 centimetres, but half of this is tail. Their flight and movements are distinctive: a rapid, flitting, undulating flight, and a twitching motion while perched. Some can sit still, temporarily.

Another common feature is the compact, beautifully made cup-like nest which they build in tree-forks and crevices. Only one genus is exceptional, the *Drymodes*.

They are all song birds, with a piping or a trilling song, with no two species singing exactly alike.

## The scarlet robin

The scarlet robin, *Petroica multicolor*, often winters in gardens or cultivated areas, sporting a bright scarlet breast under a black throat. The female is the only hen robin to have a little colour on her own breast — hers is a duller hue.

They breed from July to January in drier highland forests and woodlands. It is the female who builds the nest, while the male supplies materials and food. Several species of cuckoos foist their eggs on scarlet robins.

One courting pair were observed in an aviary: the female fluttered past the male very slowly, moving like a butterfly, barely brushing the male's head with her wings before moving on. He remained very still while she

I. R. McCann/A.N.T. Photo Library

passed and then extended each wing downwards to display the white wing patch.

This robin can be found in the southwest corner of Australia, and throughout the southeast, from Tasmania to Brisbane, from Sydney to Adelaide.

## The flame robin

The flame robin, *Petroica phoenicea*, is very similar to the scarlet robin and they often feed together in winter feeding-flocks. In the late afternoon sun on a winter's day in southeast Australia they may be seen flitting from rock to rock in open grassy areas.

*ABOVE: A pair of red-capped robins perched above their nest. Although the brightly coloured male is the more beautiful, the female's drab colour provides her with the necessary camouflage when nesting.*

The plain females and immatures usually outnumber the males, whose brilliant fronts stand out sharply. The effect in the highlands after snowfall is spectacular.

The flame robin's breast is brilliant orange, extending up the throat to leave only a chin band of grey. This contrasts with the scarlet robin's black throat. The female flame robin is

I. R. McCann/A.N.T. Photo Library

brown with a small white forehead mark.

These robins flick the wings and jerk the tail when perched, while they observe the ground before pouncing on a grub or a worm. They also feed by patrolling the ground for insects.

They nest in a cleft on a tree trunk, in a fork of branches, in building-rafters, or in rock crevices. Outwardly the nest is rough with a neat cup-shaped interior. The flame robin may breed in brown plumage.

## The pink robin

The pink robin, *Petroica rodinogaster*, displays a belly and breast of a deep violet pink, under a very dark grey throat and back. The female is rich brown above and pale brown below. As with all the ruddy breasted robins (*Petroica*), the female is the nest-builder. In this species the nest is intricate: made of moss bound with cobweb and camouflaged with lichen, all very neat and compact. It may be seen in small trees or bushes.

Like all robins, the pink robin lays three or four eggs but these may not be the eggs hatched by the hen. A cuckoo may have substituted its eggs for those of the robin.

---

*TOP LEFT: The eastern yellow robin is renowned for its curiosity. The rump of the northern yellow robin tends to be brighter than that of the southern one.*
*BELOW LEFT: The beautifully plumed rose robin lives close to water in rainforests or thickly timbered mountain ranges.*
*BELOW: The flame robin with its brilliant orange breast and grey chin band, rarely sits still for long and jerks its tail from side to side.*

R. & D. Keller/A.N.T. Photo Library

Jean-Paul Ferrero/Auscape Int.

I. R. McCann/A.N.T. Photo Library

Both these birds flit and cycle gracefully in the air. On the perch the rose robin drops and lifts its long tail.

## The red-capped robin

The red-capped robin, *Petroica goodenovii*, is the most widespread ruddy-breasted robin. It is at home in the dry interior of the continent as well as the dry, open coastal areas. Sometimes these robins forage for insects in orchards, on the wing or on the ground. They may spend much time moving among leaf-litter stirring up insects and then seizing them in a swift pounce. The nests are the usual cup-shape, camouflaged by bark and grass, subject to cuckoo parasitism.

## The hooded robin

The hooded robin, *Melanodryas cucullata*, is even more widespread, avoiding only the Cape York peninsula and Tasmania. The outstanding visual feature of the male hooded robin is its black head and throat — hence the name — coupled with a black and white body.

This robin is an actor: its distraction display is spectacular. To discourage an intruder from her nest, one female climbed a rock and rolled down it towards the observer, as though she could not fly. Being followed, she turned away and rolled over logs and rocks. This behaviour is intended to lead predators away from the nest.

The nest is typically cup-shaped, camouflaged by bark strips and built in the forks of trees. This robin is one of the few capable of long periods of stillness.

## The rose robin

The rose robin, *Petroica rosea*, is rather similar to the Pink except that its pink is brighter and its back less dark. An occasional female has a pink tinge to the underside, but the usual colour is pale grey.

The rose robin's range overlaps and is wider than the pink robin's, which is restricted to the very southeast, to Victoria and Tasmania mainly. The pink robin prefers cool, dense forest or fern-gullies; the rose robin is happy in rainforest and thickly timbered mountain ranges and is always close to water.

The nest is similar to the pink robin's but more densely covered in lichen on its outside. It feeds in the trees and thus is not often seen in the open but it is thought that some juvenile rose robins feed with the pink robins in the winter.

## The yellow-bellied robins

There are three varieties of yellow-bellied robins (far removed from the heraldic symbolism of the Robin Redbreast!) in two isolated pockets: the southwest and southeast corners of Australia. This suggests a common ancestor with a wider distribution.

In the southwest there is the white-breasted robin, *Eopsaltria georgiana*, and

*LEFT: With their soft, brown plumage, the young of the eastern yellow robin easily blend into the background.*
*BOTTOM: The grey-headed robin — seen here on its nest — is found only in northeast Queensland in mainly the tropical highland, as well as the lowland rainforest regions.*

the western yellow robin, *Eopsaltria griseogularis*, which is halfway between the white-breasted and the eastern yellow robins in the matter of yellow plumage.

The southwest birds have a restricted range. The white-breasted robin prefers dense cover, the western yellow robin prefers scrub cover. Both birds move like darts, rapidly and briefly, and then sit quite still, with minor tail movements. Both favour ground insects.

The western yellow robin appears to have arrived in the region later than the white-breasted, and is now losing its yellow, too.

The eastern yellow robin, *Eopsaltria australis*, covers the east coast from north to south, except for the tip of the peninsula. Its belly is bright yellow below the chin with the chin itself white.

It used to be thought that there were two species of eastern yellow robin; they are now classified as two races, with different coloured rumps; the northern variety is yellow, the southern is olive.

## The scrub robins

Two exceptional robins are the scrub robins. Geographically isolated from one another, they resemble each other closely.

The northern scrub robin, *Drymodes superciliaris*, lives in the Cape York Peninsula. It eats only on the forest floor, so far as is known, and nests in a saucer-shaped depression on the ground, usually lined. It has an odd, hopping, bouncing run. Very little is known about these robins.

The southern scrub robin, *Drymodes brunneopygia*, dwells in the mallee in the southwest corner and in pockets along the Bight. Its most unusual feature is that it lays only one egg in its ground nest.

Both these robins are quiet coloured with very long tails. They are the largest robins, 22–23 centimetres, nearly half of which is tail.

# LONG-LEGGED FISHERMEN

*In shallow swamps, lakes and rivers long legs are definitely an asset. There are a number of Australian birds inhabiting these wetlands that are just so equipped. Some stand over a metre high, like the brolgas and jabirus. Others, like the jacana, the moorhen and the coot, are less spectacular but compensate in toe length what they lack in leg height. All these swamp stalkers have evolved physically to suit their environment.*

## The Jabiru

Standing an impressive 1.5 metres tall on long, red legs, the jabiru, *Xenorhynchus asiaticus*, is Australia's only stork. Its head, long neck and tail are black with a glossy green tint and there's a purplish-blue patch just behind the head. The broad wings have a wide band of greenish-black on both the upper and lower surfaces, contrasting with the sparkling white of the body. The heavy bill is also black and shiny, and the eyes are yellow in the female and dark brown in the male.

Unlike many members of the stork family, the jabiru is not migratory, although it does have nomadic tendencies. It is a strong and graceful flier, with a wingspan of two metres or more, but a running leap is needed to launch it into flight. Heights of several hundred metres are often reached, slow, rhythmic wingbeats alternating with gliding and soaring flight. Unlike herons, storks are usually voiceless but jabirus sometimes utter a low booming call; they also make a clattering noise with their beaks.

The jabiru is usually seen alone, though at times wanders in casual pairs. It is common along the coast of northern Australia and occurs sparsely along the eastern seaboard to the Hawkesbury River in New South Wales; further south it is rare and only occasional vagrants reach Victoria. It also is found in New Guinea, Southeast Asia and India. Jabirus frequent swamps, mangroves and mudflats, lagoons and billabongs, sometimes

Jean-Paul Ferrero/Auscape Int.

visiting irrigated lands and other man-made water sources. Occasionally they fly off to forage in open grassy woodlands, and non-breeding birds often wander widely.

In its wetland habitat the jabiru stalks through the shallows probing for fish and crustaceans, also feeding on frogs, snakes, lizards, rodents and carrion. In pursuit of active prey, a few disjointed running steps are taken and the victim is snapped up with a forward thrust of the beak.

According to Aboriginal mythology, the jabiru was not always fond of water. A number of legends report altercations between the jabiru and the emu, and on one occasion when the two fought over food and wives, the emu threw a spear at the fleeing jabiru. The spear found its mark, came

out of the jabiru's mouth and turned into a long beak. The jabiru fell into the water and decided to stay there.

Jabiru pairs stay more or less together even outside the breeding season, which is typically from March to June in the north and August to April further south. Like most wetland species, however, they are adaptable and will wait for rain before mating. Nest building and incubation are shared by both parents. The untidy nests are large, flat piles of sticks, grass and rushes in a tree, usually near the water, and the usual clutch is two to six white eggs. The young eat food that is predigested by the parents and on hot days water is regurgitated over the chicks which sit expectantly with their beaks pointing upward. After about three months the young are

F. Park/A.N.T. Photo Library

ready to leave the nest and fend for themselves.

Jabirus have few predators although chicks are often taken by birds of prey. Unwary adults as well as juveniles sometimes fall victim to saltwater crocodiles along the river flats of far northern Australia.

# The Brolga

Long before white men ever witnessed the stately dance of the brolga, Aboriginal tribes throughout the bird's territory imitated this graceful display in their own dancing and told the story of how the brolga was created. Details of the story vary regionally but its core remains unchanged.

---

*OPPOSITE: Sometimes falling victim to crocodiles, the jabiru is surrounded by Aboriginal legend as to how it got its long beak.*
*TOP: Brolga mates with a young bird. After pairing off, the male brolga remains monogamous.*
*BELOW: The white-necked heron has the unusual trait of breeding rapidly during times of flooding.*

Bay Picture Library

There was once a beautiful young girl called Buralga, the most exquisite and expressive dancer the people had ever seen. Most women were content to play percussive accompaniment to the dancing of the men, but Buralga had to dance; not only traditional dances, but also her own. Often she went off to dance alone when her chores were done. Her fame spread far and her people were very proud of her.

Although she had many suitors she rejected them all, and one became so jealous he determined that if he could not have her, no one would. One day, as Buralga danced, he enveloped her in a magical whirlwind of dust. When the dust cloud disappeared, she was nowhere in sight and in her place stood a tall, pale grey bird such as the people had never seen. Unafraid, the bird began to dance in the same way as the missing Buralga. People called out her name and the bird seemed to understand. Then the people knew that their beloved Buralga had been changed into a bird, and thereafter this graceful dancing crane was called the 'brolga'.

The brolga, *Grus rubicundus*, can also be found in New Guinea, Asia, and occasionally, in New Zealand. It stands more than a metre in height on long, slender grey legs — the female slightly smaller than the male — and has a wingspan of 2 metres. The soft plumage is the same in both sexes and the head is bare with a conspicuous patch of red skin behind the eye.

The dancing seems to be a gregarious social activity; it may denote some courtship ritual during the October to April breeding season and off-season may serve to consolidate pairs as brolgas are monogamous. Although pairs may dance together, most of the flock usually participates, keeping time and formation throughout the dance. Aligning themselves in rows, roughly opposite one another, the birds bob their heads and bow, advance and retreat. They may leap high into the air and float down with wings outspread or toss twigs and grass stems into the air, and occasionally give sudden trumpeting calls. An adult bird will sometimes march up and down a line of young birds, apparently 'drilling' them in rehearsal. Performances lasting half an hour or more have been observed, and the birds were once reported to play a sort of 'leapfrog' over a group of bewildered cows.

Although brolgas still occur in southeastern Australia in small numbers, they are primarily tropical birds. Dense populations are found near Townsville where a flock of up to 12,000 birds has been recorded. They are common across northern Australia from Queensland to the Kimberleys, but less so further west to Onslow in Western Australia. They are also vagrant to southern New Guinea and occasionally to southwest Western Australia and even New Zealand. Drainage of swamps has drastically reduced their habitat in most settled areas, but provision of stock dams has been a boon to flocks in drier regions.

Their movements are closely related to the onset of the monsoonal wet season in October or November. When the rains start, they disperse to swampy areas where pairs nest in isolation, building unlined platform nests of grasses and stems to 1.5 metres in

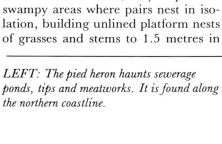

*LEFT: The pied heron haunts sewerage ponds, tips and meatworks. It is found along the northern coastline.*

Jean-Paul Ferrero/Auscape Int.

diameter or laying their two spotted white eggs on the bare ground. During the dry season they move to areas with permanent water. Some observers suggest that a pair which has successfully incubated a chick does not breed again for another two or three years, the parents and young remaining as a family unit during that time.

The brolga feeds principally on sedge tubers dug from the mud with its long, straight beak, but also eats insects, molluscs, crustaceans and frogs. During the dry when food is scarce, it may graze on sorghum, maize and other cereal crops, a habit resented by Queensland farmers.

The brolga is not a shy bird and is seen occasionally during the wet season walking around the streets of northern Australian towns. It needs a long running jump to become airborne and in flight looks clumsy with its long neck and legs extended, but it can actually fly quite long distances.

The only other crane in Australia is the sarus crane, *G. antigone* which was discovered in 1966 in association with brolgas in northeastern Queensland. It has since been found in other northern areas and may have been present in small numbers for many years, unnoticed amongst its more numerous relatives. It is a native of Southeast Asia, ranging north to the Philippines and India.

The sarus crane is slightly larger and darker than the brolga. Its legs are pinkish rather than grey and the bare red skin on the head extends further down the neck. Its behaviour and habit are similar to those of the brolga, although its dance is less spectacular and dramatic.

# Herons

There are seven species of heron in Australia, three of which are found throughout the continent and also in Tasmania. Of these three, the white-necked and white-faced species, *Ardea*

*pacifica* and *A. novaehollandiae* respectively, are quite well known, but the nankeen night heron, *Nycticorax caledonicus* is rarely seen as it feeds at night.

## The white-necked and white-faced heron

The white-faced heron is about 70 centimetres long and feeds in freshwater, seeking fish, tadpoles, crustaceans and insects. It will often move into moist paddocks to feed on grass-living insects, such as locusts, and small rodents such as mice. Large prey is usually battered against a firm object to kill it and as a way of tenderising it before swallowing.

Like many of the group, the white-faced heron takes on nuptial plumage at the onset of the breeding season. The usual grey-blue plumage remains, but is supplemented by long plumes trailing from the back and chest.

M. F. Soper/A.N.T. Photo Library

*ABOVE: The brown bittern is quite shy and normally a loner, only coming together for the breeding season.*
*LEFT: A yellow spoonbill feeds its chicks.*

I. R. McCann/A.N.T. Photo Library

One of the features which links herons, egrets and bitterns is the presence of tufts of fragile feathers over various parts of the body. Although not the only function of 'powder down' the white-faced heron uses its powder down for a very important purpose: to clean fish slime from its plumage.

Heron populations sometimes balloon in response to an increase in food supply. This is particularly true of the white-necked heron, which breeds rapidly during times of flooding. About 90 centimetres long, it is predominantly dark grey, with white face, neck and upper breast.

Whereas most of the herons tend to be quite slender, the nankeen night heron is rather squat, with shorter legs and neck and a heavier bill. Although it measures nearly 60 centimetres in length and is upright in carriage, the species appears tightly compacted and hunched.

As its name suggests, this bird is basically nocturnal, leaving its roost in a tall tree in the late afternoon for its feeding grounds in swampy areas. Although rarely seen, colonies may be found close to large cities and near suburban gardens. Many goldfish owners awake to find that their ponds have been raided by these nocturnal predators.

## The mangrove heron

The mangrove heron, *Butorides striatus*, is also a coastal dweller, but is not strictly marine. It inhabits dense stands of mangroves and nearby woodlands, searching for crabs, prawns, insects and fish. Subtropical shores are preferred, with Mallacoota on the east coast and Port Hedland on the west being usually the southern limits of its range. Standing only about 48 centimetres tall, there are two colour variations of the mangrove heron. One is grey, with a green-grey back, the other is brown with a rufous back.

## The pied and the great-billed heron

Little has been written about the two remaining heron species, the pied heron, *Ardea picata*, and the great-billed

---

heron, *A. sumatrana*. Both are birds of the northern coast, frequenters of the mudflats and waterways lined with mangroves. The pied heron also haunts sewerage ponds, tips and meatworks, or is a scavenger on the fringes of human habitation. In the wild it is basically insectivorous, though it sometimes feeds on invertebrates and small fish.

The great-billed heron is the largest of the Australian herons, reaching just over one metre in length. In flight it rather resembles a B52 — the head is tucked into the body as it lumbers and lurches on its way, in no great rush to take off.

# Egrets

Egrets are the embodiment of elegance. Their most striking feature — the long, lacy nuptial plumes — have been admired for thousands of years. Much sought after as a trim for ladies' hats, they brought many populations of the bird to the verge of extinction. Today egrets are protected in most parts of the world, allowing everyone a chance to admire their beauty.

Egrets are found throughout the world, in tropical and temperate regions.

## The white egret

In Australia there are five species, the largest of them being the large, or

white egret, *Egretta alba*. However, some ornithology authorities consider this bird to actually be a heron of genus *Ardea*, while the pied and white-faced herons previously described should be in the egret subspecies. But, in this case, the white egret will be described as part of the egret family.

The white egret is found all over Australia, except for the dry centre, and is the only common species in Tasmania.

Apart from a naked patch around the eyes, the large egret is pure white. In the breeding season it grows long filamentous plumes from the back which extend past the tail. These plumes play an important part in courtship, pair bonding and nest defence. They also highlight strategic parts of the bird's anatomy and seemingly increasing its size.

The large egret can be seen on almost any lake or estuary, patrolling the perimeter in its search for aquatic animals. Like the herons, egrets hunt by stealth, staring into the water for a sign of a fish or frog, then lunging forward with the sharp beak.

## The little and the plumed egret

Two other species of Australian egret take on beautiful plumes in the breeding season: the little egret, *E. garzetta;* and the plumed egret, *E. intermedia*. Both these species are found throughout the eastern half of the continent and into Tasmania but the former is

also found along the Western Australian coast.

The little egret is an active bird with a distinctive high-stepping gait. It hunts by stealth, but it also has another tactic: it flushes out its prey by shuffling its feet in the mud. When striking it is lightning fast, thrusting forward or twisting with a rapid movement.

Its plumes, which extend from the breast, back and nape, bear a close resemblance to those of the large egret. In the breeding season the two birds look alike, with the only distinguishing features being size and soft part colours.

The plumed egret can be distinguished from the other species by its smaller neck and yellow-green face, which is not as long as in the other species. It is often found in small groups along waterways and dams, foraging through the mud.

## The cattle egret

The fourth member of the egrets is the cattle egret, *Ardeola ibis*, which has a shorter neck than other Australian species. It is readily identified in the breeding season by the orange plumage on its head and throat. Outside the breeding season it is white.

In 1933 a group of 18 cattle egrets were released into northern Australia by pastoralists seeking to control ticks and other noxious insects. These birds may have been the forerunners of the now widespread cattle egret in Australia, for they were not present before this release. However, there is a strong possibility that the cattle egret has colonised Australia from Southeast Asia.

By whichever path the bird came, it is now found almost anywhere that cattle are raised, and also in the company of water buffalo and horses. Its survival is linked to the cattle industry, as the bird is rarely far from these beasts. It is a mutually beneficial relationship: the cattle egrets remove ticks and other parasites from the

*TOP: The white ibis is very similar in appearance to the sacred ibis of ancient Egypt; paintings and sculptures of which can be seen in Egyptian tombs and temple ruins.*
*LEFT: The glossy ibis is the smallest of the species seen here searching for frogs, snails, spiders and insects.*

cattle's backs; and the cattle flush from the grass the insects on which the bird feeds.

## The reef egret

The reef egret, *Egretta sacra*, is unique among Australian egrets in that it is confined to a marine environment. Unlike other egrets and herons it is a true seashore bird, frequenting the rocky outcrops and sandy flats along the coast.

Anatomically it is typical of its species, the body dominated by the long neck and long beak. Contrary to popular belief, the beak is not used to impale the victim, but acts rather like a pair of forceps, grasping the fish which is then either swallowed alive or battered against a rock.

The reef egret is found along most coastal areas, except those of Victoria and Tasmania. Although there is only one species, there are two distinct colour variations. In tropical waters the reef egret is generally pure white and in temperate waters blackish grey. This occurrence of two colour phases is known as polymorphism and, in the reef egret, provides no barrier to interbreeding. However, intermediate colour forms are extremely rare.

Scientists are unsure of the reason for the two colour forms. There does not seem to be any advantage in terms of hunting ability; dark egrets found in tropical areas and the dominant white variety are equally efficient.

# Bitterns

The third subdivision of the family Ardeidae are the bitterns — shy, furtive birds. In comparison with their relatives previously discussed, bitterns are stouter, quite short, and dull in colour, with none of the elegance of herons and egrets. There are 3 species breeding in Australia.

The least retiring of the group is the black bittern, *Dupetor flavicollis*. It occurs on the coast from Wollongong north and around to the southwest of Western Australia. Short, marshy vegetation offering concealment from predators is its preferred habitat.

The male will sometimes leave its cover to call from a log or stump, proclaiming its territory or attempting to attract a female. For the most part it remains under cover, quietly foraging for aquatic creatures.

The little bittern, *Ixobrychus minutus*, which reaches only 30 centimetres, is a shy bird. It inhabits reeds and dense undergrowth in and around swamps.

Like most ground-dwelling birds it is well camouflaged, its plumage consisting of browns and buffs. When disturbed it remains quite still, with the beak pointing skyward. If there should be a breeze blowing the surrounding reeds, the bittern will move in time, rocking forward and backward.

The brown bittern, *Botaurus poiciloptilus*, is the largest of the group, reaching about 70 centimetres. It too

*ABOVE: Large flocks of ibises often return to the same nesting area year after year. Ibises resemble storks and herons and belong to the same order although not the same family.*

is quite shy, but its presence is heralded — the loud booming call, very much like the mooing of a cow, usually emitted at night, can be heard several kilometres away.

The call is essential to the bittern, as contact between individuals is limited by the very nature of their habitat.

Bitterns are territorial and normally solitary, pairs only coming together for the breeding season. A territory varies greatly in size; sometimes several nests will be found in close proximity, at other times they may be widely dispersed.

Very little is known about the Australian species of bitterns, but they do appear to exhibit many of the characteristics of their European, Asian and African counterparts.

# Ibises and Spoonbills

These birds resemble storks and herons and belong to the same order, the Ciconiiformes, but not to the same family. Their family is the Threskiornithidae.

Family members are adapted for life on land and water as well as in the air, and they range widely through the temperate regions of the world. The family, however, contains relatively few species, 26 ibises and six spoonbills. Ibises are not represented in New Zealand.

In general, they are medium to large birds (75–95 centimetres tall, including the bill). All have stout bodies, long necks, short tails and long legs, terminating in feet with slightly webbed toes. The main point of difference between ibises and spoonbills is the bill. In ibises it is slender and down-curved, and in spoonbills stout and shaped at the end like a spoon.

The Australian ibis, and indeed all, species are so similar that it seems that to describe one is to describe all. There are, however, minor differentiating features. The straw-necked ibis, *Threskiornis spinicollis*, alternatively named dry weatherbird and letter

bird, occurs only in Australia. Its plumage is black with a greenish-bronze sheen; the head is black and naked; and the neck is white with thick, stiff, straw-like feathers. The white ibis, *T. molucca*, alternatively named black-necked ibis and sicklebird, also has a naked head. It resembles *T. aethiopica*, the sacred ibis of ancient Egypt, which is often represented in the sculptures and paintings found in tombs and ruined temples. The glossy ibis, *Plegadis falcinellus*, is black with maroon underparts. It is named 'glossy' but appears black from a distance, the metallic sheen on the wings being visible only at close quarters.

The royal spoonbill, *Platalea regia*, is white with black bill and legs. The yellow-billed spoonbill, *P. flavipes*, is also white with yellow legs and, not unexpectedly, a yellow bill. It is found only in Australia where it is fairly common.

Ibises and spoonbills are social animals. This sociability extends beyond

*ABOVE: A lotus bird on its nest in one of the weedy fringe areas of a freshwater lake or swamp. Note its incredibly long toes and the intricately patterned eggs.*

the family to other birds of the same order during feeding, breeding and nesting.

The main items in their diet are frogs, crayfish, fish and insects. The birds usually swallow large pieces of food whole, and regurgitate indigestible portions as pellets. Ibises probe for food in mud or solid earth using their long bills. Spoonbills gather their food while moving through water and moving their scoop-like bills from side to side below the surface. Sometimes birds of different species within the family and even within related families hunt for food together or, at least, come together after hunting to fly together to the same roost.

It is only during courtship that these sociable birds seek privacy.

While courting, some develop colour patches on the breast, head or neck, which fade as soon as a mate has been found. The male white ibis stakes out a display territory on a tree before he begins his wooing, and then tramples down bushes to make a nest. When the females arrive, the male surveys them and selects a mate. The two of them then bow solemnly to each other, a sign that a bond has been formed. With the straw-necked ibises mutual preening signifies the forming of a bond.

In the case of the royal spoonbills the female is the selector. She perches on a branch and pecks at males which approach until one she fancies arrives. Then both birds bob their head up and down.

During the breeding season the birds become social again, with groups of them coming together in a colony. Ibises and spoonbills build their nests in trees or even on the ground, usually using sticks and other vegetation. Both parents cooperate to build the nest, incubate the eggs and feed the young, the parents regurgitating food for the nestlings.

Ibises and spoonbills are one of the few groups of animals which are not threatened by man. They do not compete seriously with him for food, and they do not occupy territory which he covets. Indeed, one species, the straw-necked ibis, is named 'farmers' friend'. The bird is a travelling pest exterminator, having a strong predilection for grasshoppers and other insects which damage crops.

# The Lotus Bird

The lotus bird, *Irediparra gallinacea novaehollandiae*, is found in coastal districts from Sydney, through Queensland and across to Derby in Western Australia. The Australian subspecies is also found in New Guinea, Borneo and the Celebes. It is one of a family of seven highly specialised waders found throughout the world's temperate and tropical zones. Its habitat is swamps, lagoons and slow moving streams, chiefly those with a substantial covering of aquatic plants such as water lilies.

The lotus bird rather resembles a small plover, *Vanellus* spp.; it is about 23 centimetres in length, with black, brown and white markings. The red comb, which gives it a helmeted appearance, turns yellow when the bird gets agitated.

The most characteristic part of the lotus bird is its legs and toes, which are out of all proportion to the rest of its body. The central and hind toes each measure 7.5 centimetres, giving it a footspan of 15 centimetres.

The large feet of the lotus bird are essential, for without them it would not be able to walk across the flimsy vegetation of a swamp or lagoon. When the toes are spread they disperse the weight of only a few grams over an area of almost 200 square centimetres. With such efficient weight distribution the bird is very much at home walking over water lilies and other aquatic vegetation.

One disadvantage of the long feet is that they hinder, to an extent, the bird's flight. To lift itself from the ground it must flap the wings extremely hard to gain the initial momentum; once aloft it is by no means a powerful flier, and lands soon after takeoff.

When disturbed, the lotus bird often prefers to dive rather than fly and, although the feet are not webbed, it is a strong swimmer under water.

If there is any sign of danger it may choose to remain submerged, with just the nostrils and beak protruding from below the surface, for up to 30 minutes.

Lotus birds are normally sedentary, but birds living some distance from the coast may be semi-nomadic owing to the seasonal nature of many waterways. They are usually seen singly or in small family parties. During the breeding season the pairs become quite aggressive, and will defend their area against others of the same species.

The nest is a flimsy structure of sedge, grass and aquatic plants, built directly on floating vegetation. It is often so shallow that when the bird sits on the eggs it is level with or even below the waterline. This has no effect on the eggs, which are protected by a water-impervious layer, and are also able to float if they should fall off the nest.

The parents are attentive to the needs of both eggs and young, and have been observed carrying both under their wings to higher ground when the water level suddenly rises.

While nesting, the lotus bird is extremely wary, and will flee at the least sign of danger. If there are young in the nest, one of the parent birds performs a distraction display nearby, acting as if it had a broken wing to draw the predator away from the young.

Young lotus birds are ungainly, to say the least. One writer has described them as '. . . grotesque morsels apparently all legs and toes . . .' (J. D. Macdonald). They certainly look quite absurd; small, dark and fluffy, with legs that dominate the body.

The nesting season varies according to locality. Birds of temperate and subtropical areas usually nest between September and January; birds in the monsoonal region of northern Australia start later, from January to May.

Along the east coast the lotus bird is by no means common; but the population in northern Australia seems static, and is holding its own.

# The Swamp Hen

Found in a wide area of well-watered coastal regions and parts of the eastern interior, the swamp hen, *Porphyrio porphyrio*, is a terrestrial bird that lives in weedy, fringe areas of freshwater lakes, swamps and streams.

Belonging to the cosmopolitan family of rails or water marsh birds, the swamp hen, a shy bird, can often be seen feeding in paddocks during the day. The swamp hen will also feed in the shallower areas at dusk.

A sedentary bird, the swamp hen is capable of swimming but is rarely seen doing so. It lives in a permanent territory mainly in pairs or in a small family group. Swamp hens are adapted to walking and running and have been observed running quite fast over dry pastures.

Both sexes of the swamp hen are alike in appearance and stand about 45 centimetres tall. The upper parts of the bird, the face, neck and breast, are black-brown and have a slight gloss. The shoulders and upper belly are a rich purple. The swamp hen has a massive bill and frontal shield which is bright red along with a red eye.

Although swamp hens usually make short flights, they can surprisingly manage to fly quite long distances also: testimony to this is swamp hens having established themselves on Samoa under their own power. Some feat considering how their flight is heavy and laboured; their wings are not developed in relation to their body size. Particularly noisy at night, swamp hens can often be seen on many lakes and ponds in urban parks where some of them have become quite tame.

# Other wild hens and the Coot

Closely related to the swamp hen, the similar-looking dusky moorhen, *Gallinula tenebrosa*, is also commonly encountered in city parks. Slightly smaller than the swamp hen, and lacking the bright blue chest markings of its counterpart, the dusky moorhen occurs in a wide belt across the eastern half of Australia, with an isolated population in southwest Western Australia.

Other gallinules include the bush hen, *G. olivacea*, of northeastern Australia, and the Tasmanian native hen, *G. mortierii*. The latter once occurred over much of the mainland, but was displaced there by the black-tailed native hen probably after the land bridge between Tasmania and the mainland was flooded.

The black-tailed native hen, *G. ventralis*, is probably the most nomadic of all native hens. Although its flight is at best laboured, it is capable of travelling large distances over the Australian continent, and has even been reported completing the 3000 kilometre flight to New Zealand. Why then it has not moved into Tasmania remains open to conjecture.

Another denizen of city parks is the coot, *Fulica atra*. In general body shape, it is quite similar to the swamp hen and gallinules, but it can be easily identified by its white bill and frontal shield. Coots, too, are good fliers, and travel over all of Australia in search of suitable conditions. Most of their flights seem to take place at night, possibly in an attempt to avoid predatory birds.

*ABOVE: The dusky moorhen is a common sight in city parks. This bird is found in a wide region spanning eastern Australia.*
*LEFT: Coots are another common visitor to city parks and can be easily identified by their white bill and frontal shield.*

Nests are constructed in the swamp where reeds are suitable for bending over, intertwining and trampling down to form a platform which will support the heavy bird. Naturalists searching for the nests usually locate them among thick vegetation growth in water about one metre deep. Swamp hens have also been known in some circumstances to roost in trees and small bushes.

Three to five eggs are laid which are a pale buff colour, blotched and spotted with brown and purple. The immature birds are browner than adults and their bills and shields are a much duller red.

The swamp hen has a loud, harsh, screeching call which resembles a 'kee-oww'. When on the alert, it flicks its tail up and down in a jerky manner displaying its white undertail.

It was once thought that there were two distinct species in Australia, owing to slight differences in size and behaviour. However, it is now accepted that the western swamp hen and the eastern swamp hen are part of a single species found in Australia, Africa, Asia and Europe.

The undertail is white and the legs are either red or brown. Some birds in the southwest of the continent have a rich azure neck, breast and shoulders. In Tasmania, the swamp hen is a slightly larger bird.

The swamp hen's diet consists mainly of tender young reed stems which it bites off at the base with its strong, pincer-like bill. It then grips the reed with its large foot while it eats. Their diet is also known to include frogs and molluscs.

The breeding time of the swamp hen varies according to locality. However, nesting has been observed between January and April, in June and from August to December.

# BIRDS OF PREY

*Equipped with a sharp bill and powerful talons, birds of prey are well known for their killing ability. However, these birds — eagles, hawks and falcons — with their speed, grace and voracity have earned a special kind of respect from humans.*

The killing ability of these strong, large-winged birds has become legendary. One of their species has been known to kill lambs, kangaroos and even a horse. They are able to hover, soar in wide circles and swoop down on their victims with skill and precision.

All of Australia's birds of prey are flesh-eaters and attack their prey with a fearsome, sharp, hooked bill and powerful talons. Their speed, grace and voracity as well as their distinctive appearance has earned them a special kind of respect from mankind.

They are especially noted for their dramatic powers of flight. Some species are expert at gliding and soaring on air currents although all tend to rely on the more conventional flapping flight over short distances.

From as early as the eighth century BC, hawks, eagles and falcons were trained to hunt game. Falconry was widely practised in Europe and Asia and was traditionally a leisure pursuit of the wealthy, often organised under royal patronage. Enthusiasm for the sport has fluctuated over the centuries but interest has been revived in recent years.

Birds of prey have characterised features which evolved in adaptation to their plundering lives. The sharp, hooked beak, made to tear flesh or plumage, varies in size and strength according to diet. Their usual food

*J. Brownlie/A.N.T. Photo Library*

*RIGHT: The letter-winged kite is so known because of its underwing markings. As with all birds of prey, it has strong, powerful talons and a sharp hooked beak. The letter-winged kite lives in the open dry interior of Australia.*

ranges from insects, frogs, lizards, snakes and fish to rodents and small animals. They prey on many creatures regarded as pests, but larger species are also noted for their attacks on livestock, poultry and game.

The toes are the principal weapon and most dangerous feature of these birds. Three digits face forward and one backwards, the hind toe commonly being the heaviest and strongest. The size and shape of the body, wings and tail are also adapted to each bird's preferred habitat and most common method of flight, even among those that hunt from a perch.

The plumage is dense and the feathers large and strong. In most soaring species and also, non-soaring species, each feather can bend individually, like a separate wing, to provide added control. Some of the more trimly proportioned kites and kestrels use this form of flight regularly, even when hunting.

Forest-dwellers generally have relatively short wings which increase their manoeuvrability between trees. Those best adapted for effortless soaring, such as the eagle and osprey, have long, broad wings which are in optimal proportion to the size and weight of the body. Falcons which rely on rapid flight have a heavy, pointed body which gives them maximum momentum when diving.

All birds of prey have very acute vision. This is due to their relatively large eyes and to the remarkable density of the cones or visual cells on the retina. They also possess both binocular vision (as in humans) and monocular vision (as in most birds), which is made possible by the existence of two foveae (pits forming the points of sharpest focus on the retina) in each eye, one pointing forward and one directed sideways. They do not have the highly developed hearing of owls, but do hear acutely in the low-frequency range. Forest species generally have larger earholes than species of open country.

Hunting techniques vary widely according to habitat and food preferences. Some species take their prey on the wing, some attack on the ground and others in water. Many kites and eagles rob other birds of their captured prey, and harriers frequently prey on nestlings. Food is usually captured in the talons: small prey taken in flight is transferred to the beak immediately and eaten without landing, but larger victims are transported to a perch and eaten at leisure.

In the case of carrion, a meal may be eaten on the spot or chunks of flesh torn off and carried away for consumption. When prey is taken from the ground, the bird's outstretched legs are retracted quickly on contact and the talons closed tightly: combined with the impact of the diving bird, this usually crushes the prey.

Most birds of prey perform majestic aerial displays, soaring in high, wide circles on thermal currents. At the onset of the breeding season, the osprey will plunge dive, regain height and repeat the performance again and again, soaring up to 350 metres above the ground.

The kite often glides gracefully for short distances with its wings held straight and in a wide V-shape. The male of the little eagle will fly rapidly upwards at a steep angle then fold its wings and plummet down, repeating this manoeuvre many times while calling loudly.

As elsewhere in the world, Australia's birds of prey prefer grasslands and open woodlands although hawks and goshawks are among the inhabitants of forests where they prey on hapless birds and insects. Many species are found throughout the continent but some have a more restricted range. The elegant letter-winged kite usually stays close to the grassy plains of the dry interior but like its close relative the black-shouldered kite may visit coastal districts. Ospreys, brahminy kites and sea eagles occur only around the coast: the brahminy kite, also known as the red-backed sea eagle, is restricted to the northern half of the continent but the true sea eagle extends its range into southern river systems.

Since their introduction to Australia, rabbits have become an important source of food for most birds of prey. Animals as large as wallabies and medium-sized kangaroos may be taken by the larger species, such as black-breasted buzzard and wedge-tailed eagle. Black-breasted buzzards have also been reported to break emu eggs by dropping rocks on them.

The osprey is one of the few birds of prey that build their nests on the ground. Most construct them in trees or, in the case of other coastal species such as the sea eagle, on rocky fore-

*ABOVE: The little eagle, unlike the larger species, takes its prey from the ground, and will either eat its victim on the ground or else move it to higher ground.*

shore and cliffs. Some birds, including the brown falcon which is common throughout Australia, takeover the abandoned nests of other birds.

Like other creatures, birds of prey are threatened by the destruction of their habitats but the most serious threat to their survival has been the widespread use of insecticides. Accumulating in the bird's body these affect the formation of the egg shells, making them thin and fragile so that many are broken during incubation.

Birds of prey are long lived, the usual life span being around ten years but some species have been recorded as surviving into their twenties.

# The Wedge-tailed Eagle

Australia's largest bird of prey is the wedge-tailed eagle, *Aquila audax*, a majestic bird with a wing span of up to 2.5 metres — well over the length of a man. Unofficial measurements of wing spans giving figures of 3.3 metres have been claimed, but these can not be verified. Nevertheless even with a 2.5 metre wing span this makes the wedge-tail the fourth largest eagle in the world.

The majesty of the wedge-tailed eagle is fully realised on the open plains, when it soars and wheels on outstretched wings, buoyed by the thermal currents. This eagle is known to glide for as long as 90 minutes, performing marvellous aerobatic displays, at heights of well over 2000 metres.

Wedge-tailed eagles rarely reach the speeds of the smaller hawks, kites and falcons, but they are quite mobile and very competent at swooping on a darting rabbit.

The talons are exceptionally strong, and as the bird descends on its prey (a rabbit, kangaroo or wallaby perhaps) they can exert a pressure of three tons — more than enough to snap a man's wrist. And if that is not sufficient to kill the victim, the powerful beak comes into play to finish the job.

Unlike many of its counterparts around the world, this eagle seems to have thrived from the changes European settlement has brought. Land clearance and the introduction of new food sources have allowed the wedge-tailed eagle to increase its extent and density across Australia. It now occupies forest areas and plains throughout the mainland and Tasmania.

The wedge-tail breeds from June to August in southern Australia, and a little earlier in the north. In drier areas they may not breed for several seasons if conditions are not favourable. A large platform of sticks, lined with leaves, in the fork of a tall tree forms the nest.

Normally two eggs are laid, but unless conditions are exceptionally good only one chick will survive. The parent birds are extremely territorial, and will defend the nest and surrounding area against any other eagle. The chick fledges when it is about 85 days old.

Young birds are nomadic, and will travel great distances in search of a territory. One fledgling banded at Canberra was shot eight months later at Cunningham, Queensland, 864 kilometres away. Often the juveniles will group together, working their way along river valleys. It is probably these

Bay Picture Library

*ABOVE: An enemy of the house mouse, the black shouldered kite doesn't soar as such but instead beats its wings rapidly when flying and hovers.*

juvenile flocks that have caused farmers and hunters to shoot them in great numbers, fearing for the safety of their sheep and lambs.

The wedge-tailed eagle has come in for a great deal of criticism over recent years for its alleged predations on sheep. In its defence, conservationists have claimed that it takes very few live lambs, and generally only those that are sick. They also point out that the eagle does the pastoral industry a great service by destroying great numbers of rabbits. Though this last claim is open to conjecture, there is no doubt that the wedge-tailed eagles' persecution has been based more on ignorance and myth than on facts.

In 1969 it was estimated that 30 000 birds were being shot annually. Most areas had declared it to be vermin, many placed a bounty on its head. The wedge-tailed eagle was more often seen strung up on a wire fence than in full flight.

Today the wedge-tail numbers seem to be secure, despite the widespread attempts at eradication that were undertaken in the past. The wedge-tail is now protected in all states, and killing of them is only allowed under very special circumstances.

The cause of the persecution was the belief that the wedge-tail was responsible for attacks on lambs. Since the early 1970s many studies have been carried out, and show quite clearly that the wedge-tail is of no threat to the pastoral industry.

In Carnarvon, Western Australia, a study conducted over three lambing periods followed the movements of eleven eagles. Over the three periods, when lambs were in plentiful supply, only two were killed.

Similar results have been obtained around Australia. Certainly eagles will feed on dead lambs, but these have nearly always died from other causes. When a lamb is actually killed by an eagle it is generally a sick or injured lamb.

The percentage of lambs killed that would otherwise have survived is extremely small and of no consequence to the economic viability of sheep farmers.

Even though in some areas rabbits may make up 98 per cent of the wedge-tailed's diet, the wedge-tailed eagle has little overall impact on rabbit populations. Studies have shown that at times when rabbit kills are at their highest, this corresponds with a high rabbit population boom.

At Rawlinna, Western Australia, for example, it was found that eagles killed 9 rabbits per square kilometre; but the population density was between 160 and 170 rabbits per square kilometre.

Only in areas of small rabbit populations, and during drought, does the wedge-tailed eagle have a significant impact.

Where there are no large rabbit populations wedge-tailed eagles must turn to more traditional food sources. The variety of the diet is amazing — anything from small thorny lizards to good sized kangaroos are taken. Carrion is often consumed, including dead domestic stock — hence the belief that wedge-tailed eagles are stock killers.

The wedge-tailed eagle has been the victim of over-zealous persecution in the past, and how it has recovered its former numbers is nothing short of a miracle. It is a truly beautiful bird of

*BELOW: The majestic wedge-tailed eagle was severely persecuted and hunted in the '60s and '70s, but is now again secure in numbers.*

Bay Picture Library

prey, one that should instil respect and admiration — not condemnation and killing.

# The Shortwings

The true hawks are distinguished by short, relatively broad wings, a long tail, slender body and long bare legs. Known to falconers, or more correctly austringers, as 'shortwings', they are birds of the woodland, skulking amongst the foliage to suddenly dart out and snatch a passing bird, dashing through bushes to flush and grab prey or gliding effortlessly down on an unwitting rabbit. Typically, they sit quietly, using a perch as a vantage point from which they attack prey, a technique known as still-hunting.

In Australia we have three true accipiters or shortwings: two goshawks, the brown goshawk, *Accipiter fasciatus*, and grey goshawk *A. novaehollandiae*, and a sparrowhawk, *A. cirrhocephalus*. A fourth species, called the red goshawk, is thought by most to also be an accipiter. At present it is in its own genus, *Erythrotriorchis*, and is at best an aberrant goshawk. Amongst other unusual characteristics it has long wings, reaching almost to its tail tip. Whatever its relationship to other goshawks, it is unique to Australia and considered one of our most rare and endangered birds.

When more than one accipiter occurs in an area, which is often the case, size differences help them coexist by feeding on different size classes of prey. Where all four of Australia's 'goshawks' live together they form an eight member group ranging in size from the massive female red goshawk to the tiny male sparrowhawk. Each has its own place not only because of its size, and thus the size of prey it is able to catch, but also because of slightly differing hunting techniques, hunting areas, nest site preferences and times of nesting.

Once a year all of the hawks build a flattish platform of sticks, with a central, leaf-lined cavity in which to lay their eggs. Alternatively, they may refurbish their previous year's nest. The two larger birds, the red goshawk and grey goshawk, usually lay 2 eggs, the two smaller birds lay 3 eggs. Their eggs are white, sometimes with a few small brown speckles; they have little

need for camouflage as the parents incubate and protect them almost continuously.

Male grey goshawks and female brown goshawks, which are similar in size, have bred together in the wild, producing hybrid offspring. This does not seem to be a common occurrence and may be due to the habitat changes wrought by man. Where once the two goshawks, although sometimes found in the same area, were separated by differing preferences for food and nest sites, clearing and opening up of forests and introduction of prey such as rabbits and starlings may have broken down the barriers.

Have you ever heard the frantic piping voice of a lone honeyeater hidden in a bush, or watched a flock of starlings bunch together and, as one, plunge earthwards, or a noisy group of galahs suddenly spiral upwards in a tight group? Their behaviour signals the presence of a hawk. Searching skywards you may spot the cause of the commotion but more likely you will see nothing and wonder at the fuss. The culprit may well be lurking unnoticed by you in the foliage of a nearby tree. Such is the nature of goshawks.

Although common and often frequenting our suburbs and city parks they are seldom noticed. Nevertheless, at times they make their presence painfully obvious to aviculturists, pigeon fanciers and the owners of poultry by their sometimes reckless and persistent attempts to get a seemingly easy meal. They will follow pigeons into their lofts, reach with long legs through the wire of a cage dragging as much of the hapless victim out as possible, or simply cause such terror in their intended quarry that it injures itself flying frantically against the sides of its cage.

The goshawks though, are doing what comes naturally. It is of little comfort to the owner of several dead chickens, but it is unlikely the attackers, often adult birds, will stay in the one place for long. The goshawks will soon give up and move on if they catch nothing. In the meantime, it is wise to keep the chickens caged and the finches shielded from the sight of hawks. Mirror balls placed at corners of bird enclosures are said to be a totally effective deterrent to hawks. Goshawks have learned to live with us, so surely we can learn to live with

*ABOVE: The grisly remains of a wedge-tailed eagle's meal, a rabbit. Although rabbits can be a major portion of a wedge-tailed eagle's diet, studies have shown that these birds have little impact on rabbit populations.*

them. They are handsome, fearless hunters and useful creatures, as any viticulturist who has seen a goshawk scattering the starlings destroying his grapes will testify.

Although the effects of humans have reached all parts of Australia, the true accipiters have, on the whole, adapted well. The brown goshawk and collared sparrowhawk even thrive in cities and the grey goshawk will frequent farmland. The somewhat atypical red goshawk seems unable to cope with the encroachment of man. Until more is known about it, its future depends on the continuing existence of large areas of undisturbed northern woodland.

## The red goshawk

The red goshawk inhabits the woodlands of north and northeast Australia within about 300 kilometres of the coast. In historical times it was found as far south as Sydney but now is all but absent from New South Wales.

Although never common, habitat change, particularly clearing, is thought to be the main reason for its decline. The few nests that have been found in recent times have been in undisturbed woodland. It is much larger and more conspicuous in habits than the other goshawks and would find it difficult to live unmolested in close association with man. With a wingspan well over a metre, colourful rufous, barred plumage and a relatively slow deliberate flight it is a difficult bird to miss. Perhaps significantly, the first description of the red goshawk was made from a painting of a skin nailed to a settler's hut

Little is known of the red goshawk's habits. Their massive legs and feet, and long middle toe, indicate that they catch large birds. They have been seen catching or eating wood ducks, cocka-

J. & L. Cupper/Auscape Int.

toos, kookaburras, rainbow lorikeets, a half-grown hare and a frilled lizard.

Like all the goshawks, the red goshawk is sexually dimorphic in size; the female is larger than the male. Dimorphism is particularly evident in bird catching species: the more birds in the diet the more difference in size between the sexes. This is thought to reduce competition between male and female allowing them to live together in an area that would not always support two birds of the same size. The male catches, on average, smaller more agile prey than his mate.

## The collared sparrowhawk

The male collared sparrowhawk, so named because of the rufous ring around its nape, is the smallest and most delicate in appearance of Australia's birds of prey. The size of the Australian mudlark, with a wingspan of only 75 centimetres and matchstick-thin legs, he is a bolder hunter, daringly snatching small birds and insects from the air.

Like the other accipiters he catches prey using stealth and surprise. The sparrowhawk will approach a flock of feeding starlings with a short burst of high speed, hugging the ground and bursting upon them virtually unseen, or it will stalk its prey through the bushes. It is widespread, occurring throughout Australia and also in New Guinea, but preferring woodlands of the semi-arid zone.

## The brown goshawk

The brown goshawk can be found almost anywhere there are trees. Often

*ABOVE: This red goshawk parent and chick are finishing off the remains of a laughing kookaburra.*
*RIGHT: A brown goshawk removing a hatched egg shell from the nest.*

confused with the sparrowhawk, the brown goshawk is a larger bird with a wingspan of slightly less than a metre. Although similar in colour — both hawks are brown backed with a vertically streaked front in their first year and grey backed with a horizontally barred front in subsequent years — they can be distinguished by the shape of their tail. Brown goshawks have a rounded tail tip, whilst that of the sparrowhawk is square or blunt. At close range there are also other differences: the goshawk has a protruding brow, giving it a frowning,

J. & L. Cupper/Auscape Int.

J. & L. Cupper/Auscape Int.

fierce expression; the sparrowhawk lacks this heavy brow so that it is button-eyed and more innocent in appearance.

While both goshawk and sparrowhawk have long 'bird-catching' toes, the latter has a proportionately longer middle toe reflecting the fact that it catches most of its prey in the air while the goshawk catches some on the ground.

## The grey goshawk

The closely related grey goshawk is only found in the 750 millimetre rainfall zone of northern and eastern Australia, including Tasmania, and also in New Guinea and Melanesia. Unlike the brown goshawk and sparrowhawk, it does not nest in cities but will nest in farmland. It occurs in two interbreeding colour forms, soft pastel grey and

J. & L. Cupper/Auscape Int.

32

R. & D. Keller/A.N.T. Photo Library

dazzling white. Both colour morphs (forms) have canary yellow legs and, as adults, deep red eyes — a striking combination. The only pure white bird of prey found outside the arctic, its pale plumage may blend in flight with the bright sky and shiny leaves of the closed forest it often inhabits, or allow it to fly, as has been observed, undetected in a flock of sulphur-crested cockatoos.

White goshawks eat birds, mammals, reptiles, insects and occasionally carrion. The heavier grey goshawk is a less aerial hunter than the brown goshawk and hunts less in the open. It catches large pigeons, brush turkeys, bandicoots and other prey amongst the trees. The introduction of rabbits to Australia has provided an extra, abundant food source for both goshawks in southern Australia, perhaps allowing them to increase in numbers.

# The Falcons

Among the Falconidae family, is the peregrine falcon, one of the swiftest and deadliest birds of prey and traditionally favoured by falconers. It is a killer of racing pigeons and rabbits and swoops on its prey at verified speeds of 180 kilometres per hour. Also in the falcon family is the nankeen kestrel which is often seen around towns on the outskirts of aerodromes in undeveloped wasteland areas.

# The Sport of Falconry

Practised by ancient man as early as 700 BC, the sport of falconry has survived the passage of time and in recent years, due to magazine articles and television programs has enjoyed a revival.

Originating in the Middle East and the Orient, the sport was introduced to Europe by travellers and adventurers who brought a number of birds and their masters back to Europe with them. Falconry became widespread and immensely popular throughout Western Europe and gained a reputation as a sport for the privileged classes.

Falconry suffered a decline during the 1600s due to the prominence of hunting with a shotgun. In Great Britain the Falconers' Society of England was founded as early as 1770 but ceased operations in 1838. The main headquarters of European falconry was then centred in the Netherlands under the patronage of King William II of the Netherlands. The modern British Falconers' Club was founded in 1927. Clubs were formed in a number of other countries including France, Germany, Austria, Italy, Japan and the United States. In Australia, however, the sport of falconry is illegal.

The sport has gained many adherents since World War II. The sheiks of Saudi Arabia and the Persian Gulf states still train their falcons to hunt bustard. Falconers in India and Pakistan train their birds to hunt ducks and partridges while Japanese birds of prey hunt for pheasant.

After the bird is trapped, training begins by carrying the bird on a heavily gloved fist for several hours a day. During this time, the bird is spoken to softly and its plumage stroked gently with a feather.

When the bird is able to feed from the fist without its rufter or eye covering, it is then deemed ready to be broken to people. It is then trained to feed from a lure: a padded weight with wings attached, to which meat is tied. The lure is whirled around and the bird trained to fly to it aggressively over increased distances. Once this practice is mastered, the bird is then trained to kill for itself and is presumed ready for hunting.

# PARROT PARADE

*The parrot family is big; there are around 332 species in it. Among the species are rosellas, lorikeets, cockatoos, galahs and bugerigars, all of which can be seen in the wild, in sanctuaries and within the confines of an aviary. These colourful birds continually delight with their noisy chatter, clowning antics and enthusiastic eating habits.*

Parrots have a number of common names which sometimes cause confusion and misunderstanding. Among our Australian parrots take, for example, the lovely crimson rosella. The name is this bird's current and 'official' name but many aviculturists and bird watchers insist on calling it the mountain lowry, red lowry, mountain parrot or Pennant's parakeet. Is it then a parrot, lowry, lory, rosella or parakeet? Of course, it *is* a parrot and it *is* a rosella, but most serious bird watchers and ornithologists would now agree that it is certainly not a lowry, lory or parakeet. All members of the group of birds known as parrots can correctly be called parrot, but we give some groups of parrots a different common name for convenience, so that they are more comprehensible as smaller, related groupings.

Just as all mammals, including human beings, belong to the animal class Mammalia, so all birds belong to the class Aves. The 9000 or so living species of birds within Aves are divided into 29 orders of birds. The 332 species of parrots of the world all belong to the one order of birds, the Psittaciformes. Many of the 29 orders of birds consist of several or many families, but the parrot order Psittaciformes contains only the parrot family, Psittacidae. This is because the parrots constitute a very distinct group of birds closely related to each other but not very closely related to any other group of birds. Their closest relatives are thought to be the pigeons.

Within the single parrot family Psittacidae the 332 species are thought to form three subgroups or subfamilies, and these are helpful in sorting out the confusion caused by common names of parrots in Australia.

The first parrot subfamily is the Loriinae which, as one would easily guess, contains all of the colourful noisy parrots commonly known as lories or lorikeets. In the past these lorikeets have also been called parrot, lory, mountain parrot, keet, leek, greenie, jerryang, gizzie and zit parrot. All these odd names should now be disused, however, in favour of the more appropriate and correct 'official' suffix of lorikeet. This is only in Australia; outside this country the name lory is most predominant.

## Lorikeets

There are around six or seven species of lorikeet in Australia. They are colourful birds, mostly green with touches of red about the head, from 15 to 35 centimetres long, with the tail making up approximately one-third of their length. Their bill is short and deep and, when open, reveals their most distinguishing feature, a brush-like tongue. They use this to lap up the nectar of eucalypts and other flowering trees. Their short legs terminate in feet with two toes pointed forward and two backward. Bills and feet each have a double function: they are used to hold food and to climb.

It would seem that the rainbow lorikeet with its bright, gaudy colouring would be most conspicuous when feeding in a blossom-covered tree. This is not so. Amid the brilliant colouring of the flowers the lorikeet is completely camouflaged. The breast and sides of rainbow lorikeet, *Trichoglossus haematodus*, are yellow barred with blue; the outer wings are green and blue; and the wings at the base of the wing feathers are orange.

Contenders for the title of

Jean-Paul Ferrero/Auscape Int.

*ABOVE: Rainbow lorikeets are true comics of the birdworld with their antics. Their colourful plumage surprisingly serves as camouflage when feeding in blossom-covered trees.*

'fairest' would include the varied lorikeet, *Psitteuteles versicolor*, also called the red-capped lorikeet. It is a spectacular bird with dark-red forehead and crown, green back and tail and yellow breast. It ranges along the northern coastline of Australia.

The musk lorikeet, *Glossopsitta concinna*, is another rival for the title. It is mostly green, with a black bill tipped with red. Its range extends along the southeast and southern parts of Australia, including Tasmania. The purple-crowned lorikeet *G. porphyrocephala* is a third contender. It has a purple forehead, orange ear covers and a green body. It inhabits the

southern part of the continent from east to west.

The little lorikeet, *G. pusilla*, while not the fairest is certainly the smallest, only 155 millimetres long. Its face is red, the upper body green, and the underparts are yellow. Its range covers southeastern Australia.

Lorikeets roost in the limbs of trees in the vicinity of water. At sunrise they leave the roost for their favourite eating place, usually a field rich in nectar-filled blossoms. They also fancy grain and orchard fruits, and so are something of a menace to farmers and orchardists.

Emily Post who wrote on etiquette in the twenties would have considered their eating behaviour uncouth, and it must still be considered uncouth in the eighties. Neville Cayley describes it: 'They are exceptionally greedy feeders, gorging until the feathers of their heads, necks and breasts are a sticky mass, and the nectar pours from their throats.'

Lorikeets are born clowns. Mischievous and inquisitive, some of their antics are as funny as an old Laurel and Hardy movie. They can even mimic human speech; this talent is confined to tame birds. Lorikeets in

*ABOVE: Feeding on pollen, nectar and fruit, the purple-crowned lorikeet ranges over most of southern Australia.*
*BELOW LEFT: The varied lorikeet, also called the red-capped lorikeet, is found along the northern Australian coastline.*
*BELOW RIGHT: The musk lorikeet, rather subdued in colour when compared to some of the other members of its family has a mostly green body and a black bill.*

the wild chatter noisily, but they do not mimic other creatures.

These birds can easily be encouraged to make themselves at home in your garden, but to do so is to invite the displeasure of neighbours who enjoy the sounds of silence. The noise level of a rock group is low compared to the racket made by a chorus of screeching lorikeets.

If you would like to establish a lorikeet aviary, Neville Cayley recommends the rainbow lorikeet, but with reservations. 'It is extremely active, twisting, turning and climbing on the perches ... The pairs display a marked attachment to each other, often playing together for hours; their courtship is accompanied with much dancing and bowing and droll antics.'

He adds, however, that because of 'its activity and particularly the liquid nature of its droppings, it should only be kept in large aviaries.'

At Currumbin on Queensland's Gold Coast a property owner, Mr. Alex Griffiths, found that the lorikeets were eating his flowers. To divert their attentions from the flowers he dotted his garden with honey pots. The lorikeets approved of this new food source — and they told their friends and relations about it. Now 2000 lorikeets drop in daily for a meal, and thousands of visitors drop in to watch them feeding. Tourist attractions are seldom established so undesignedly.

# Cockatoos

Another parrot subfamily is the Cacatuinae, far better known as the cockatoos. These large, powerfully billed, and raucous parrots are represented in Australia by 11 species. Seven of them, the palm, black (including both the yellow and white-tailed), red-tailed, glossy, gang gang, sulphur-crested and Major Mitchell's, are called cockatoos while two others are known as corellas, one a cockatiel

*TOP: Twittering away on their perch, these little lorikeets are often very hard to see because of their small size and colouring. RIGHT: The scaly-breasted lorikeet has habits resembling those of the rainbow lorikeet. These two species often occur together in mixed flocks.*

D. & M. Trounson/NPIAW

in a hollow limb, where one or two eggs are laid. Incubation is undertaken by the female, who is fed by the male during her time at the nest.

The young, when they hatch, are naked and helpless, and will stay in the nest for about 10–12 weeks before venturing into the outside world.

Large numbers of black cockatoos were taken for the pet trade before controls were introduced. Generally, the young were removed from the nest and raised by hand.

If the nest was inaccessible, then the whole tree was cut down — a practice which effectively diminished the supply of nesting sites for future seasons. Today, the black cockatoos are fully protected, but destruction of habitat is still a threat as more areas are cleared for agriculture.

## The palm cockatoo

The king of Australian parrots is without doubt the palm cockatoo, *Probosciger aterrimus*, of Cape York. It is the only member of its genus, and is also called goliath cockatoo — quite appropriate considering its size and strength.

Individuals have been measured at nearly 70 centimetres — 10 centimetres bigger than the familiar sulphur-crested cockatoo!

The beak of the palm cockatoo is incredibly strong. Captive specimens quickly shred metal containers, and have even been known to bend cyclone wire fencing, the only material strong enough to restrain them.

Handling these birds is obviously a risky business, and several fingers are known to have been parted from their careless owners. In the wild the massive beak is an essential tool in extracting the seeds of the pandanus palm, which lie deep inside a protective cover.

The palm cockatoo is distinguished by its glossy black plumage, large crest, and a naked cheek patch which blushes to bright red when the bird becomes excited. Distribution is confined to the rainforests of Cape York, some offshore islands and New Guinea.

and the last is the famous galah. The last four are smaller than most cockatoos and are a little different to the more typical cockatoos and this is why they have different names. But they are all considered to be members of the cockatoos, even the cockatiel which is considerably smaller than the others in its group and rather different in its colouration.

All members of the subfamily Cacatuinae have an obvious erectable crest on the crown and have a relatively large to huge bill which is capable of cracking and tearing seed or tree wood. Such names or name suffixes as parrot, juggler, cocklerina, chockalott, quarrion or weero have been used for some of these birds.

The black cockatoos are divided into three genera — *Probosciger*, *Calyptorhynchus*, and *Callocephalon*. All are characterised by a dark or black body, strong beak, and legs and feet well adapted to gripping.

Nesting is carried out high in a tree,

Bay Picture Library

Pandanus seeds make up a great deal of the palm cockatoos' diet, but they also feed on nuts, fruit, leaf buds, and wood-boring larvae. This liking for larvae is common among the black cockatoos and is another reason for the strong beaks.

The larvae may be several centimetres inside a tree, and a good deal of strength and dexterity is required to extract the tasty morsel.

The nesting habits of the palm cockatoo have not been studied greatly: although generally quite approachable, during the breeding season the bird becomes intensely secretive. This lack of knowlcdgc has hampered attempts to breed the palm cockatoo in captivity, something essential for its survival.

Habitat loss has already diminished its range, and any further significant clearing of the rainforests could see it wiped out.

## The yellow-tailed black cockatoo

Fortunately the position of the other black cockatoos is more secure. One, the yellow-tailed black cockatoo, *Calyptorhynchus funereus*, has even benefited from European settlement. Although it has suffered from habitat loss, pine plantations have given it a new and expansive source of food.

An inhabitant of eastern Australia from Central Queensland to the Eyre Peninsula in South Australia, the yellow-tailed black cockatoo favours well watered areas that support large tracts of forest.

It is, perhaps, the best known of the black cockatoos, and its large dark brown and black body, yellow cheek patch, and characteristic yellow band across the tail are unmistakable.

The yellow-tailed black cockatoo was one of the first known to early settlers and earned the name of funeral cockatoo because of its dark plumage and long drawn out whistle — a call that gave it the Aboriginal name of wylah.

D. & M. Trounson/NPIAW

*TOP: The yellow-tailed black cockatoo relishes pine seeds, and at times thousands of them can be seen carpeting the floor of a pine foresting dissecting pine cones.*
*LEFT: Casuarina tree seeds are a favourite for the unobtrusive glossy black cockatoo.*

*ABOVE: Major Mitchell's cockatoos, with their pink and white colouring.*
*TOP RIGHT: The male gang-gang cockatoo bears a bright red head and crest; the female lacks this colouring.*

The famous naturalist John Gould noted that its flight was 'rather powerful, but at the same time laboured and heavy'. When feeding, however, it displays exceptional talents of strength and agility, being equally adroit at dissecting pine cones for their seeds and extracting grubs from infested trees.

The yellow-tailed and white-tailed black cockatoos share a liking for pine seeds, and at times thousands can be seen blanketing a forest, grasping a pine cone in one foot and clinging to a swaying stem with the other.

Foresters at first saw the birds' depredation on pine cones as a threat to the industry, but realised that the birds' habit of dropping a large number of unopened cones to the ground would make seed collection a much easier task.

Both species do the timber industry a great service by feeding on wood-boring larvae. A good deal of timber is saved, and the spread of these pests is slowed significantly simply by allowing these cockatoos to take the place of harmful pesticides.

## The white-tailed cockatoo

A close relative of the yellow-tailed black cockatoo is the white-tailed black cockatoo, *C. baudinii*, of southwest Western Australia. In fact, the two are so similar that some ornithologists choose to treat them as one species. This move, however, has not gained widespread acceptance, as there are some distinctions between the two.

The white-tailed black cockatoo has a white cheek patch and white bars across the tail. It often moves about in large flocks, while the yellow-tailed species is seen in small groups of 2–10 birds. The white-tailed cockatoo has adapted to the drier areas, as well as the wetter, forested districts, and are now thought to be two different species rather than a variation within one species. The forest species tend to have a longer, narrower beak to extract seeds from their capsules, while birds of the dry inland tend to have a shorter, heavier beak to crush the cones of banksias and hakeas.

During the summer months the long-billed birds often congregate in large flocks in forested areas, returning once again to the inland before the winter rains.

Aboriginals and white settlers knew of this movement and looked forward to the birds' approach as a signal of the coming rains. Aboriginals, who called the white-tailed black cockatoo Ngol-yë-nuk, even included a few of its feathers in rain-making ceremonies.

## The red-tailed cockatoo

The most widespread of the black cockatoos is the red-tailed black cockatoo, *C. magnificus*, a highly nomadic bird which ranges, at various times, across northern Australia, into western Victoria and west to Adelaide. It is about the same size as the yellow-tailed and white-tailed species — 50–60 centimetres.

BELOW: *Perhaps the most well-known of cockatoos, the sulphur-crested cockatoo lives in forests, woodlands and scattered heavy timber areas in open country, especially near water.*
RIGHT: *A young galah staring cheekily out of its nesthole.*

The body is black, males being considerably darker than females and possessing the distinctive red tail bars. Females have yellow-orange tail bars, and yellow flecks on the head and shoulders.

Although wooded areas are preferred by this species, it is not averse to feeding on the ground in more open areas, and often helps in the control of certain pasture weeds, such as the double-gee, *Emex australis*.

Seeds, particularly casuarina, marri and hakea, are commonly eaten, and at times the birds will also take nectar and berries.

The red-tailed black cockatoo has the distinction of being the first Australian parrot to be sketched by a European. In 1770 the draughtsman Sydney Parkinson, assistant to Joseph Banks on the *Endeavour*, made a pencil sketch, but unfortunately the intended painting was never completed.

## The glossy black cockatoo

Often confused with the red-tailed black cockatoo is the glossy black cockatoo, *C. lathami*; at a distance, the two are quite similar. Close observation is difficult, as it is an unobtrusive and suspicious bird, but when examined at close range the differences between the two become apparent.

The glossy black cockatoo is about 5–10 centimetres smaller than its counterpart and the female has a much yellower head. In addition, the glossy black cockatoo does not have a crest — the only black cockatoo without this feature.

The glossy black cockatoo is also known as casuarina cockatoo, because of its almost exclusive preference for seeds of the casuarina tree. This preference becomes obsessive in cap-

Bay Picture Library

R. & D. Keller/A.N.T. Photo Library

*LEFT: The crimson rosella and . . .*
*ABOVE: The yellow rosella. Rosellas can*
*be distinguished from other Australian*
*parrots by their blue, white or yellow cheek*
*patches, mottled backs and broad long*
*graduated tails.*

tivity, and thwarted early attempts by aviculturists to breed them.

It was not until the late Sir Edward Hallstrom, Chairman of the Taronga Zoo Trust, went to great lengths in 1954 that success was achieved. Hallstrom was plagued by a lack of casuarina trees — a problem which today confronts the glossy black cockatoo in the wild — and he and his employees had to drive many miles each day in search of suitable seeds.

Attempts at preserving the glossy black cockatoo in the wild, centre around re-establishing large stands of casuarinas, such as on Kangaroo Island, off the South Australia coast.

## The gang-gang cockatoo

One of the more spectacular of the cockatoos, and the most confiding, is the gang-gang cockatoo, *Callocephalon fimbriatum*. It is in a genus on its own, like the palm cockatoo, but its dark plumage places it under the general heading of black cockatoos.

It is the smallest of the group, 35 centimetres, with white edging on its grey feathers. The male is distinguished by a bright red head and crest; the female lacks this bold marking.

Gang-gangs inhabit the southeast corner of Australia, occasionally making vagrant crossings of Bass Strait to King Island and Tasmania. Mountain forests and valleys are preferred, especially during the breeding season, after which many birds move into the lowlands for the winter months.

The remarkable tameness of this bird always delights naturalists, some of whom become too unsuspecting and receive a nasty nip for their complacency.

Suburban areas have opened up new feeding possibilities for the gang-gang and it relishes a meal of soft berries. Gang-gangs also eat the seeds of eucalypts and acacias and the larvae of various moths and insects.

The sight of a party of gang-gangs foraging among snow-laden branches is in stark contrast to the majesty of a palm cockatoo soaring high above the rainforest canopy, and bears testimony to the marvellous success of our cockatoos.

# The Galah

Galahs are one of the most abundant and familiar of all Australian parrots. Medium-sized birds growing to about 35 centimetres in length, galahs are grey above but have a rosy chest and underparts and a white or pink crest. Their bill is bluish white and the legs dark grey, the eyes are dark in the male and pink in the female. Renowned for their beauty and also their ability to mimic the human voice, galahs are popular pets.

*RIGHT: The eastern ringneck parrot inhabits woodlands.*
*BELOW: King parrots live off seeds, mainly fruit seeds, honey and insects. These parrots have a high-pitched shriek.*

*ABOVE: The turquoise parrot is closely related to the scarlet-breasted parrot. It can either be a solitary or gregarious bird.*

The galah is one of the few native Australian creatures that has benefited dramatically from European settlement and cultivation of the land. Before British colonisation they were rare, east of the Great Dividing Range but are now found over most of the continent, including Tasmania and some offshore islands. Only in quite recent times they have become established along the eastern seaboard and in the southern half of Western Australia. Observers have noted that galahs vacate the far north of the Northern Territory during the worst of the wet season but are common there at other times. In arid regions they remain fairly close to water sources.

The great extension in range and burgeoning of numbers is largely due to the growing of grain, the increased provision of water for stock in arid regions, the opening up of habitats, and irrigation schemes which ensure a virtual year-round supply of food. Typical birds of open forest and grassland, galahs are mainly seed-eaters and have taken quite readily to introduced cereal crops. They appear to be particularly partial to wheat and oats, but have also developed a taste for the seeds of pasture grasses and oilseeds such as sunflower and safflower. To round out their diet they eat roots, foliage, flowers, nuts, fruits and insects.

Like most cockatoos they are considered pests in grain-growing districts as they invade growing crops as well as harvested seeds. Their depredations have been held responsible for the demise of oilseed cropping in the Wimmera district of Victoria and it is estimated that cockatoos destroy about one-fifth of the total grain crop in New South Wales each year. Galahs are protected in Australia.

Galahs provide some benefits, too, as they eat large quantities of the seeds of many weeds. Although they occur in greater number in agricultural districts, galahs have made themselves at home in urban areas as well — feeding in parks and gardens, on golf courses and sports fields, and even nesting in street trees.

They feed in flocks of usually 30 to 100, which are made up either of pairs

Bav Picture Library

(which usually mate for life) or of non-breeding younger birds.

Occasionally these join together and flocks of many hundreds may be formed. Galahs are fond of aerobatic displays, which are incorporated into courtship rituals but also performed daily before roosting and during rainstorms. These are accompanied by much swooping through the treetops (or telegraph poles) and loud, raucous screaming.

# Rosellas and other Parrots

The third subfamily of parrots, the Psittacinae, is by far the largest and it is within this larger and more diverse group that common names are often confusing to the unwary or unfamiliar. To avoid what has been a very long-term problem, the Royal Australasian Ornithologists Union and the world's parrot authority, Joseph M. Forshaw of Canberra, have suggested names that should replace the numerous and often misleading names previously in common or local use.

The greatest confusion within the last subfamily is caused by the names rosella, parrot and parakeet. Rosellas are all very closely related and belong to the one genus (*Platycercus*). The rosellas are found only on the Australian mainland and Tasmania. They can be distinguished from other Australian groups of parrots by their obvious blue, white or yellow cheek patches, heavily mottled backs and broad long graduated tails.

All of the remaining species of Australian parrots have the suffix of parrot, such as night parrot, rock parrot and paradise parrot except the famous budgerigar, and the bluebonnet (which is also called the bluebonnet parrot).

*ABOVE: Two newly hatched budgerigar chicks wait in their nest for food to arrive from the parents. In 30 days time these chicks will be ready to leave the nest and soon after, will be independent.*

# Budgerigars

Dainty parrots that come today in blues, lutinos, albinos, pieds, harlequins, and even spangled varieties, these housebound budgerigars are all far removed from the original stock. The wild budgerigar is predominantly green, with earth-brown bars along the back of the head and the dorsal region.

The forehead and cheeks are yellow, with a patch of violet in the cheek. Males and females are almost identical, except for the cere (the skin at the base of the beak) which is blue in the adult male and brown in the female and juvenile.

Juveniles can be further distinguished by the brown bars which extend all the way to the cere, and contract to the top of the head as they mature.

The budgerigar, *Melopsittacus undulatus*, is another of the Australian parrots. Prolific in numbers, it is found throughout inland areas west of the Great Dividing Range across to the Western Australian coast. It is a highly nomadic bird, covering huge distances in search of suitable habitat.

Open woodland is its preferred habitat, within reasonable distance of a water supply. In the early morning and towards evening budgerigars descend on a creek or waterhole and drink deeply in the pigeon fashion. During hot spells, especially with the midday sun, they settle in the trees' foliage for hours on end.

In particularly good areas they may stay close to the waterhole all day, but more often they are forced to fly off to search for food. This is predominantly

seeds and herbaceous plants. They eat a great deal of soft herbs as well as consuming shellgrit and sand to aid in the digestive processes.

Breeding depends to a great extent on the availability of food, but as a general rule June to September is preferred in the north, and August to January in the south. After rain in the centre they will breed quickly and raise several broods in succession.

A hollow tree limb provides the nesting site, and is lined by fine woodshavings that are probably chewed from the interior of the hollow by the parents. Only the female incubates the four to six small white eggs — the male makes regular visits to the nest to supply her with food.

After 18 days the eggs hatch, and after a further 30 days the young are ready to leave the nest. They are independent soon after and will join the flock that steadily grows in size as the breeding season progresses.

The size of budgerigar flocks is

almost legendary in the outback. One report from Paratoo Station, near Broken Hill, in 1932 stated that one huge flock started to fly over about 5 am. The sky darkened, and the screeching flock passed over continuously until 8 am. It was impossible to calculate how many birds were in the flock, but it must have been many millions.

Flocks of such magnitude, of course, are quite rare, but it is relatively common to see flocks of several thousand birds. When they descend en masse upon the branches of a dead tree it appears that the tree has suddenly come back to life with a burst into blossom.

The large flocks sometimes belie the true status of the budgerigar, for in times of drought these birds suffer greatly. Many thousands die on the

*ABOVE: Budgerigars — perhaps the most popular of the parrot species to be set up in aviaries. They make excellent pets and become quite tame.*

fringes of drying waterholes — up to 60 000 were recorded on one occasion.

In captivity budgies make excellent pets, and become quite tame. They are wonderful mimics and, with a little patience on the part of the owner-instructor, they can develop an extensive repertoire.

Contrary to popular belief, females can mimic just as well as males, however they do require more patience. They tend to be a little more agressive, and take some time to settle down. Without soft herbs and shellgrit in their diet, captive budgies tend to look like poor images of their wild counterparts.

Once they become tame, budgerigars love nothing better than to fly around the house, and when accustomed to this they will often return to their cage with a minimum of prompting.

In some countries there have been attempts at keeping budgerigars in a free-range state, much as pigeons are kept. The birds are let out daily for a few hours, and return at an allotted time, usually by putting out some food for them.

This idea has had varying degrees of success, some breeders doing very well while others have let their flocks out, never to see them again. Perhaps it will not be long before we have homing-budgie races, or maybe budgerigars could provide Telecom with a cheap means of long-distance communication.

# THE MOUNDBUILDERS

*Most of the birds in this chapter build mounds for the purpose of incubating their eggs. The lyrebird, however, builds his mound or platform as a stage on which to perform his courtship dancing and songs. The origins of the true moundbuilders and the lyrebirds are thought to be entirely different but both species have a fowl-like appearance and both are construction engineers.*

## The True Moundbuilders

Amongst the many marvels seen by early travellers in the southern hemisphere was the existence of birds which constructed incubators. The phenomenon was first reported, quite accurately, by Antonio Pigafetta who observed such birds in the Philippines during his voyage with Magellan in the early sixteenth century. Subsequent visitors to those islands also described the birds, usually with fanciful exaggeration. But it was another 300 years before this seemingly improbable avian habit was granted credence when, in 1821, John Latham published the first official description of the Australian brush turkey. It was first named as such by J. E. Gray in 1831.

There are about thirteen species of mound-building birds, all but one inhabiting tropical or subtropical regions. The brush turkey, *Alectura lathami*, and the mallee fowl, *Leipoa ocellata*, are found only in Australia. The scrub fowl, *Megapodius freycinet*, occurs also in the islands of Torres Strait and the South Pacific. The remaining species are restricted to South Pacific islands such as Samoa, the Marianas, the Philippines, Sumatra and the Nicobar Islands in the Bay of Bengal.

With chickens, pheasants, quails and allied species, moundbuilders form the order Galliformes of ground-dwelling birds characterised by having three free front toes and a short hind toe. They belong to the family Megapodiidae and all have brownish-black plumage and large strong legs and feet.

They range in size from the small scrub fowl, which reaches about 40 centimetres in length, to the brush or scrub turkey which may grow to 70 centimetres. They generally resemble their relatives, particularly hens, peacocks and pheasants, having the same fan-like tail and habit of pecking the ground to feed.

The incubating mounds built by megapodes vary greatly according to

---

*BELOW: The brush turkey has a bright red neck with yellow wattles and is confined to the east coast of Australia.*

species and local conditions. Those inhabiting areas where there is volcanic activity merely bury their eggs in the warm soil and forget them. Others use the warm sands of tropical beaches or lodge their eggs in the crevices of sun-warmed rocks and cover them with leaves. Forest-dwelling megapodes such as the brush turkey heap damp vegetation matter into mounds which generate heat during the process of decomposition, removing some of it when the temperature rises too high and adding new material when it drops too low.

Although some species maintain the mound to ensure optimum temperature control, they take no notice of the eggs. Hatchlings dig themselves out of the ground, taking from two to fifteen hours to reach the surface, and are immediately able to fend for themselves. Already fledged, they can fly only hours after hatching — a feature unique amongst birds, as is the lack of parental care. A pair of mound-building birds, on the other hand, mate for life.

The question of why the megapodes go to all this trouble, rather than just sitting on their eggs as other birds do, has intrigued ornithologists for many years.

The other popular theory is that such incubation is a specialised development of more conventional brooding habits in adaptation to particular environmental conditions. This hypothesis is supported by the fact that some jungle-dwelling megapodes still build primitive incubators resembling sand- or soil-covered nests.

A similar incubation practice occurs among crocodiles and other saurian reptiles but their mounds are of extremely simple construction and the temperature is not regulated.

## The scrub fowl

The scrub fowl occurs in Australia along the northern coastal fringe from the Kimberleys in Western Australia to Yeppoon, Queensland. It is a dull-brown bird with a bluish-grey neck, throat and chest.

Its nesting and mound-building habits vary according to local environmental conditions: along the coast its mound generally consists of sand and only a little vegetable matter. Both the male and female participate in building and maintaining the mound, which often reaches five metres in diameter.

## The brush turkey

The Australian brush turkey is confined to the east coast from the tip of Cape York Peninsula to northern New South Wales. It resembles its more familiar namesake and has a bright-red neck with yellow wattles.

The male is a strict overseer of the mound and the presence of the female is permitted only for the purpose of mating or laying her eggs. The male checks the temperature of the incubator mound by digging a hole and thrusting his head inside.

The same mound is often used year after year by scrub fowl and brush turkeys. In such cases the mound may become huge, one having been nearly 20 metres long, 5 metres wide and 3 metres high. Early European settlers in northern Australia thought these knolls were Aboriginal burial places.

The old rotten core of the mound is cold, as is the upper layer where fermentation has not yet begun. Eggs are laid only in the actively decomposing layer, by burrowing into the mound.

## The mallee fowl

As its name suggests, the mallee fowl inhabits the arid mallee scrub country of western New South Wales and Victoria, South Australia and southern Western Australia. This species has grey, brown and white speckled plumage, and grows to about 60 centimetres in length.

It is generally accepted that the mallee fowl and the brush turkey share a similar ancestor.

When central Australia was heavily timbered and well watered, the ancestors of the brush turkey and the mallee fowl ranged most of the continent and built mounds of organic matter in the forests.

After aridity set in about 20 000 years ago, the mallee fowl gradually developed its present camouflaged plumage and idiosyncratic mound-building technique.

The bushes and shrubs of mallee regions have few leaves and when these fall they quickly wither and are blown away. Even if the sparse ground litter is heaped, it is moist only during winter rains, drying and blowing away in spring.

Thus no heat-generating fermentation can occur and to overcome this problem the mallee fowl buries damp vegetation as a leaven and seals the mound with sand.

In a habitat where, even in midsummer, daily temperatures may fluctuate by more than 15°C the mallee fowl is kept busy building and adjusting its incubator throughout the year.

Work on a new mound begins around April or May and continues almost daily until breeding is finished in the following March. Mounds are usually based on the remains of previous heaps, although fresh ones may be dug on a convenient rabbit burrow or other existing hole.

*BELOW: If living in coastal areas, the scrub fowl's mound generally consists of sand and a little vegetable matter. The scrub fowl has a dull-brown coloured plumage with a blue-grey neck, throat and chest.*

R. & D. Keller/A.N.T. Photo Library

Old debris is removed and tossed aside, including any newly hatched chicks or unhatched eggs which may still be in the mound, and the hole is enlarged to about a metre deep by 3 metres across.

Dirt is piled crater-like around the rim. The leaves, twigs and even branches up to a metre long are swept into rows which the bird then scratches into the crater with its feet. Such material as hessian and barbed wire has also been inadvertently included.

Mound-building is determined by rainfall. During wet autumns an early

*RIGHT: A male mallee fowl working on its mound. Mounds are filled with vegetation and then sealed to provide the necessary temperatures for incubation of the eggs. BELOW: A mallee fowl mound.*

*LEFT: The lyrebird is one of the most gifted mimics, being able to reproduce the sounds of machinery, musical instruments as well as the noise of other birds and animals.*

chamber — about 30 centimetres wide and 30–60 centimetres deep — is filled with a mixture of fine leaves and sand.

Sand is continually kicked over the organic material in the mound until the layer is up to a metre thick. The male checks the temperature of the egg chamber almost daily, watched by an anxious female.

Though both participate in mound preparation, once it is complete the male takes over supervision and maintenance.

Adult males are strongly territorial and have associated calls and displays. During the brief period between the end of a breeding season and preparation of a new mound, pairs cease holding territories and may gather in small groups.

With the resumption of mound-building activity they re-adopt a territory, though not necessarily the same one held in the previous season. Mound-building by young birds seems to be largely unsuccessful, proficiency developing with practice. Poorly built mounds are subject to desiccation and to depredation by foxes and reptilian predators.

Later in the season the mallee fowl uncovers the mound to supplement the waning fermentation process with the sun's heat, recovering the mound at night. When fermentation ceases they depend entirely on solar radiation.

Incubation takes forty-nine or fifty days, eggs being laid intermittently during the season according to rainfall and fermentation rates. Clutch size varies enormously with the weather, from none during drought up to thirty or more in good seasons.

The mallee fowl is still abundant in parts of its range, but the overall population and distribution have greatly decreased. There is some predation by foxes on the eggs as well as the birds, but the grazing of sheep in the inland scrub strikes at the food supply of the birds and thus constitutes a far greater threat to their survival.

start is made, old mounds being emptied and renovated with frenzied haste. If autumn proves arid the pits are filled with dry vegetation and the birds wait for rain.

Unlike the local wheat farmers, who plant their crop in anticipation, the birds do no further mound work until the rains come and will not lay eggs if conditions are wrong. Once the organic matter in the pit is wet, it is covered with sand so that fermentation begins.

Like the brush turkey, the mallee fowl checks the temperature in the mound by digging a hole and sticking his head through it with mouth agape (the tongue is the receptor organ).

By about August, when the mass is already heating, an egg chamber is dug in the centre of the mound. Any large sticks are wrested out and the

# Lyrebirds

Lyrebirds are among Australia's best-known native birds, even though they are rarely seen in their natural habitat. Their fame rests securely on three distinctive qualities. First, and most obvious, is the striking beauty of the male bird's huge, lyre-like tail when it is held erect and fanned out in display. Second is the display itself, which consists of prolonged singing and dancing or prancing about on a platform stage which the male constructs for this purpose. Third is the lyrebird's astonishing mimetic ability. Not only do lyrebirds render with great fidelity the individual songs of other birds and the chatter of flocks of birds, but they also mimic the sounds of other animals, human noises, machinery of all kinds, explosions and musical instruments.

Lyrebirds are not the only Australian birds capable of such imitations, for at least sixty native and four introduced species are known to practise mimicry, but lyrebirds are undoubtedly among the most accomplished. Some birds merely echo sounds as they are heard and promptly forget them, not adding them to a permanent repertoire, but lyrebirds command an extensive range of stolen songs and other sounds, in addition to their own song and calls, which are used repeatedly and regularly long after they were first heard. In addition, the young birds learn from their elders. The range of sounds imitated is much more restricted during the breeding season than at other times.

Display in adult males is restricted to the breeding season, but juvenile males may be seen practising at other times. The superb lyrebird, *Menura novaehollandiae* which breeds between May and October but primarily in June and July, occurs in eastern forests from Melbourne north as far as Queensland's southern border, and from the coast inland to around 1500 metres on the eastern slopes of the Great Dividing Range. This species was successfully introduced into Tasmania about fifty years ago.

Albert's lyrebird, *M. alberti*, a rare creature, lives only in a small pocket of subtropical rainforest on the border between Queensland and New South Wales and breeds in June and July. This bird's displays are performed on a platform constructed by trampling

*ABOVE: A male lyrebird during his courting display. The male bird fans out his tail and brings it over his head, often obscuring the rest of his body.*
*RIGHT: The mound of a scrub or jungle fowl.*

down thorny lawyer vines or other dense growth, while the superb lyrebird scratches up a flat mound of earth. These theatrical arenas are nearly a metre wide and about 15 centimetres high.

During his song and dance routine, which may last up to half an hour, the male fans out his long tail and brings it forward over his head so that his body is often entirely obscured from the front. The two long lyrate feathers, one on either side, frame a dozen filmy filamentous feathers sprayed out between them. In the centre, two long, slender plumes cross one another and arch gracefully upward. The tail feathers are brown on top so that the folded tail is rather drab, but the

Jean-Paul Ferrero/Auscape Int.

*LEFT: A female lyrebird flying to the nest. Visits from the male to the nest are rare. The female will build the nest, incubate the eggs and then search for insects, grubs and small animals to feed itself and the growing chick.*

Doubtless this clue was also once used by feather collectors, but this practice has now been outlawed and lyrebird plumes no longer adorn women's hats. Interestingly, these lace feathers were rarely used as adornment by Aboriginals.

At the very young age, the lyrebird chick is able to emit a powerful scream. This it does at the slightest disturbance of the nest, to defend itself when escape is impossible and to bring about the speedy arrival of the mother. As lyrebirds breed in winter, they avoid most of the active predators which prey on the eggs and hatchlings of other bird species.

Outside the breeding season, groups of several birds, both mature and immature, are seen together, but it is not known whether these are family groups. Lyrebirds feed on small insects, worms and grubs by scratching with their large feet in the leaf litter on the forest floor and digging deeply into the rotting wood of fallen logs.

Adult males of both species are between 80 and 90 centimetres long but their bodies are only the size of a domestic fowl and more than half of their total length is in the tail. Female birds are about 65 centimetres long and have comparatively short tails which they do not fan. As their wings are short, lyrebirds fly only occasionally. More commonly, the wings are used to assist the bird in gliding between rocks and trees.

Lyrebirds dwell in damp, dark forests, especially in gullies and ravines, and being shy and difficult to approach are seldom observed, although in some places they live quite close to settled areas. An exception to this is the population resident in Sherbrooke Forest near Melbourne where the birds have become accustomed to human presence and seem relatively tame.

Individual lyrebirds, too, have been kept in a semi-domesticated state. When they are actively taught, these birds usually show remarkable facility for mimicry and usually acquire a far larger repertoire of sounds related to human activity than do those in the wild.

undersides are silvery-grey, giving a shimmering quality to the inverted fan. The tail of the Albert's lyrebird is less spectacular than that of his superb cousin, but his display is equally striking.

When the female, attracted by the display, approaches the platform, the male stops singing and makes a gentle clicking sound. One male may mate with numerous females, but gives no assistance with nest building, incubation or the rearing of young, although he seems to know where nests are located.

Lyrebird nests, domed with a side entrance, are constructed of sticks and roots and lined with moss, ferns and feathers. They may be located on the ground, on stumps, in tree ferns, on rocks or on rock ledges on cliff faces. Each female lays only one egg per season. The egg — purple with brown and black streaks and blotches — hatches after six weeks, and the chick remains in the nest for another six weeks. During this time the mother not only feeds the chick but also removes its droppings from the nest. Neatly packaged in gelatinous sacs, they are dropped into nearby water or, if there is no water in the area, are buried. This behaviour is presumably aimed at eliminating a scent which might attract predators.

The presence of these pellets in pools or at the edges of streams — a sure sign that a nest is located nearby — is used by scientists and birdwatchers in tracking their quarry.

51

# THE WEBBED-FEET BRIGADE

*Geese, swans and ducks are ideally suited to their aquatic life, having thick, waterproof plumage; large, flat bills and webbed feet. Their webbed feet make moving around on swampy land easier and they also work as paddles in the water. The feet of the grebes are not exactly webbed; rather they are 'lobed', having fleshy parts around each toe. The magpie goose, too, has only partly webbed feet. None of these birds are swift on land but in or around water they are perfectly at home.*

## Ducks

Australia's ducks belong to the world-wide waterfowl family Anatidae, which also includes geese and swans. We have 23 species, of which two are introduced species and two are infrequent visitors from the Northern Hemisphere.

Compared to the large numbers of waterfowl found elsewhere in the world — Great Britain alone has 47 species — Australia is not particularly well-endowed. It has been speculated that this could be due to the unpredictable nature of rainfall over much of the continent.

In the Northern Hemisphere, with its regular, seasonal climate, ducks have adapted to an annual movement between breeding and wintering grounds. In Australia though, no such pattern is possible. Ducks will inhabit an area while it provides food and shelter, then move on to a new area, perhaps returning only in several years time.

Breeding, too, depends on rainfall, and the food it provides. Only those species that inhabit areas of regular rainfall, such as the monsoonal north, maintain a regular breeding cycle. Most species wait until the swamps and billabongs begin to fill before breeding, and others, such as the pink-eared duck, *Malacorhynchus membranaceus*, will not breed until floodwaters rise over the riverbanks.

When conditions are favourable, ducks will breed at an astronomical

Bay Picture Library

A. & S. Tingay/A.N.T. Photo Library

*LEFT: A pink-eared duck preens itself with its bill.*

*BOTTOM LEFT: The common wood duck has an easily recognised mournful call.*

*ABOVE: A flock of grass whistle ducks roaming for food. These ducks nest on land at the fringe of water and eat land vegetation, mainly grasses.*

*RIGHT: A black duck guards her brood. Perhaps the best known of ducks, the black duck can be found in almost every lagoon, swamp or billabong.*

rate; clutches of up to 15 eggs are quite common. Such a huge breeding potential is vital, since duck mortality is very high — most will not live more than 12 months, and very few live to the maximum age of between eight and ten years.

The first sight newly hatched ducklings have of the outside world varies between species, but for some it must be frightening. Many species, such as the wood duck, *Chenonetta jubata*, nest in tree hollows, which may be several metres above the ground. For the fortunate ducklings, the necessary leap will end in a soft plop into the water; others not so fortunate must land directly onto *terra firma* — their first initiation into the school of hard knocks.

B. Chudleigh/A.N.T. Photo Library

53

R. & D. Keller/A.N.T. Photo Library

Bay Picture Library

Ducks are devoted parents, and will often go to extreme lengths to protect their young. It is not uncommon for them to take on intruders many times their own size if the safety of their young is in jeopardy.

For those ducklings lucky enough to survive the early months, their life will be one of constant moving between wetlands, searching for new sources of food. Soft grasses and herbs are the usual food, and varying amounts of small insects and molluscs. Some, like the pink-eared duck, *Matacorhynchus membranaceus*, feed on tiny algae, which is filtered through lamellae in the bill.

Not all ducks are fond of water — the grass whistling duck, *Dendrocygna eytoni*, for example, is usually seen on the land. It is an awkward swimmer, and appears much more comfortable grazing on grassy plains. During the day it camps in groups around the edges of lakes and swamps, before flying up to 30 kilometres at dusk to its feeding grounds.

Australia's duck species range from the bizarre to the beautiful.

Perhaps the best known species is the black duck, *Anas superciliosa*, which in some areas is a true nomad, ranging over the entire country; in other areas it is sedentary; and yet in others, is more or less migratory. Almost every lagoon, swamp or billabong has its share of black ducks. It is the favourite bird with hunters, and during the hunting season large numbers are

*TOP LEFT: Black ducks, like wood ducks, cautiously guard the nest. These nests are sometimes built in tree hollows.*
*TOP RIGHT: The mallard interbreeding with the black duck could seriously threaten the genetic structure of the black duck in Australia.*

shot. The black duck does not seem to have suffered greatly from man's predation, but it is under threat from within its own family. Interbreeding with the introduced mallard, *Anas platyrynchos*, could seriously weaken the genetic structure of the black duck population, rendering them unable to withstand Australia's erratic climate. The risk is in black ducks becoming sedentary, like their mallard cousins, and losing their nomadic instincts.

However, a greater threat to the future of the black ducks is the replacement or genetic swamping of them, as is the case in New Zealand. In New Zealand mallards are well on the way to replacing the black duck — a situation that must not occur in Australia. Mallards can out compete black ducks in areas and cause them to lose their genetic integrity.

In contrast to the colour of the black duck is the rare and beautiful white pygmy goose, *Nettapus coromandelianus*, of northern Queensland. This unobtrusive little bird is also found in Southeast Asia, and prefers deep lagoons with a large amount of aquatic plants. Though its numbers are not

great, and its range extremely limited, the white pygmy goose does not seem to be in any danger of extinction at the moment. As long as its habitat is left intact it should continue to delight those fortunate enough to see it.

The most flamboyant of Australian ducks is the musk duck, *Biziura lobata*. The male, with its overpowering smell of musk emitted from the preen gland on its rump, indulges in an extravagant courtship display that involves kicking up jets of water with its feet. During this display the pouch under its bill becomes inflated, swelling the throat and cheeks. An excellent example for the old saying 'like a duck out of water', the musk duck is helpless on land compared to when it is in the water where it is quite at home. It is an excellent swimmer and diver, choosing to escape detection by submerging all but its nostrils and eyes, or else by submerging completely and swimming away below the surface.

Almost all our ducks are threatened by increasing human settlement. The draining of wetlands for development poses the most obvious threat, for this destroys the birds' habitat. But other, less obvious intrusions are occurring. Water management schemes, controlling river levels and preventing floods, often remove the impetus needed for many species to breed. The white-eyed duck, *Aythya australis*, for example, will not breed until it is sure that the swamps and billabongs will be fully replenished. If the water does not rise enough, as often happens, it simply will not breed.

The draining of permanent swamps on coastal areas also has a dramatic effect on waterfowl numbers. During prolonged droughts these swamps provide vital refuges, where thousands of birds congregate until rains fall inland. With the great reduction in the number of permanent coastal wetlands, duck populations have decreased significantly.

A few species have benefited by the arrival of European man. The grass whistling duck is one, for it prefers the man-made pastures of the tropical north. The green pygmy goose, *Nettapus pulchellus*, is another, an aggressive but beautiful inhabitant of the far north. Though some of its habitat has been lost, it has benefited by the provision of permanent water for stock and irrigation.

Fortunately all our ducks are either fully protected, or their hunting is closely controlled. However, a few of the species, including the Burdekin duck *Tadorna radjah*, and the freckled duck, *Strictonetta naevosa,* are seriously threatened by hunters, the latter because it is rare, and the Burdekin duck, because it is taken illegally in large numbers — despite its being fully protected and not particularly good eating.

If Australian waterfowl are to survive into the future a nationwide management programme must be developed before it is too late. Suitable habitat, both on the coast and inland, needs to be provided so that our ducks can rebuild their diminished populations. And if the black duck is to continue as a popular game bird, then steps must be taken to ensure its rival, the mallard, does not make any further inroads into the black duck population. Hopefully, with the right moves, the future will become somewhat brighter for our ducks.

# Swans

Early European settlers were easily bewildered by many 'strange' Australian animals. One source of great fascination was the discovery of a black swan, *Cygnus atratus*, first spotted by Dutch navigator Willem de Vlamingh in 1697 on what is now known as the Swan River of Western Australia.

All the swans known to Europeans had been white; many legends and traditions had grown up around the aristocratic white swan. So understandably, news of the Australian black swan was received with scepticism.

There is really nothing peculiar about black swans other than their

*BELOW LEFT: Mallards nest close to swamps, laying about eight to ten glossy eggs.*
*BELOW: The male musk duck's lobe of flesh hanging from its throat becomes inflated when it performs its courting display.*

blackness, which is relieved by white wing tips, clearly visible in flight, and an orange-red beak with a white bar near the tip. They are scientifically classified in the same genus as white swans and are closely related to the mute swan, *C. olor*, which was introduced to Australia from the northern hemisphere in the nineteenth century. But they occur naturally only in Australia, where they are found throughout the southern third of the continent, along the east coast as far north as Townsville, and in Tasmania.

They gather in pairs or family groups, or congregate in flocks numbering several hundred, on any large, permanent lake or swamp such as the Coorong in South Australia and Moulting Lagoon in Tasmania. On the east coast they are common in the southern tablelands of New South Wales and in coastal swamps as well as frequenting brackish water such as Lake Macquarie near Newcastle. Black swans are vegetarians, grazing on water plants and on pastures near the water.

Because they are unusual and beautiful, black swans have been introduced to many other countries and are kept in aviaries all over the world. The first exportation was by the Dutch who took three specimens to Batavia, all of which died shortly after landing. In New Zealand, however, where they were introduced in the 1860s, black swans acclimatised rapidly and are now so numerous in some areas of the South Island that they are considered pests.

The myth of a 'swan song' — the belief that a swan sang a song of death as its life was about to end — is Greek in origin and many people still subscribe to it. Swans certainly do sing while living and the songs of the sexes are quite distinctive, the call of the male being deeper and longer. Some people find the trumpeting call of the black swans quite musical, but the explorer George Bass likened it to 'the creaking of a rusty alehouse sign on a windy day'.

Black swans build large, rather haphazard nests near the water's edge and, where they nest in colonies, regularly pilfer each other's nest materials. If an egg goes astray in this confusion, it will be 'adopted' by another swan which will push it into its nest and incubate it. Most clutches contain between three and nine eggs, pale bluish-green but turning brown with nest stains before hatching 39 to 43 days after being laid. In older birds, pair bonding is permanent until one of the partners dies. Both parents incubate and rear the brood. In younger birds, which start breeding at about 18 months of age, promiscuity is common and one parent may abandon its partner to mate again, leaving only one parent to incubate and rear the young. In this way up to four broods may be raised by a single female in a season. The downy, light grey cygnets enter the water as soon as they are hatched, swimming and feeding and occasionally climbing on a parent's back for a rest.

Each year between September and February black swans moult their flight feathers and are very easily caught while flightless, being normally relatively fearless. Swans with young are also easy to catch as they will not, even when threatened with death, abandon their brood. A similar devotion exists between the male and female of a permanent pair. This easy prey was heavily exploited last century and huge quantities of birds were taken for their feathers. They were also sometimes eaten, although they are reportedly not very tasty. Today, however, the black swan is a protected

*RIGHT: The white-eyed duck or hardhead eats mainly aquatic vegetation and lives in fresh water, preferably long flat stretches of water.*

species and is abundant in most suitable areas.

# Cape Barren Geese

It was first reported in 1792 by the French naturalist Jacques-Julien Houten de Labillardière who chose to classify it as a species of swan: 'This species is somewhat smaller than our wild swan, and of an ash-coloured grey . . .' The French zoologist Vieillot first imagined the bird to be the offspring of the black swan, but later decided to call it a goose.

George Bass sighted Cape Barren geese on islands off the Victorian coast in 1797, and the birds were later classified by the leading English ornithologist, John Latham, who proposed the creation of a new genus, *Cereopsis*. Latham ignored the vernacular name of 'goose' completely, referring to it as the New Holland Cereopsis, and the scientific name of the species has remained, since 1801, *Cereopsis novaehollandiae*. Later it acquired the common name Cape Barren goose, in reference to one of its habitats, Cape Barren Island in Bass Strait.

It is easy to see why this distinctive bird caused so much confusion. It

shares some of the characteristics of the true geese of the northern hemisphere as well as resembling swans and the shelduck, a type of large duck. But it is sufficiently different to warrant a separate classification. For this reason, it is placed in a tribe of its own, Cereopsini, in the subfamily Anserinae which includes geese, swans, the freckled duck and tree-ducks.

The Cape Barren goose has one of the smallest populations of any waterfowl in the world, numbering about 11 000. Its habitat is limited, being confined to the islands off the southern coast of Australia, including the Furneaux Group northeast of Tasmania; the islands off Wilson's Promontory, Victoria; those of Spencer Gulf and adjacent areas in South Australia; and Recherche Archipelago in Western Australia. Many birds also visit the southern mainland coast of South Australia and Victoria, generally in summer. It is believed that a relative, now extinct, once inhabited New Zealand.

When mature, this bird stands to a height of about 85 centimetres: the long neck, erect head with alert, hazel-brown eyes, and relatively long legs give it a dignified appearance. The body, about a metre in length, is predominantly ash-grey in colour with scattered black spots on the shoulders. The head is a paler grey with a white crown, while the tail is black above

and grey beneath; the feet are black. Contrasting with these muted tones, the adult bird has two splashes of colour: its legs are a pinkish shade and the cere which covers most of the short, black bill is a greenish-yellow. Both sexes are generally quiet while on the ground, but in flight the female often makes a low-pitched grunting noise and the gander a fairly high-pitched, rapid honking.

The Cape Barren goose is a terrestrial bird, favouring tussocky grasslands amongst granite boulders,

---

*LEFT: The green pygmy duck is one of the few duck species which has not suffered from human habitation. It lives in permanent water for stock and irrigation as well as its more untouched habitats of lagoons and swamps with lakes with swamp vegetation.*
*BELOW: The Radjah shellduck or Burdekin duck is severely threatened by hunters. It gathers in groups at the edge of water and on mudbanks. It is not often seen on the water.*

*LEFT: The black swan which occurs naturally only in Australia, is easily identified by its white wing tips and orange-red beak.*
*ABOVE: From 39–45 days after the eggs are laid, fluffy cygnets will hatch.*
*RIGHT: The large Cape Barren goose lives in pockets along the southern Australian coastline and northern Tasmania.*
*BOTTOM RIGHT: Cape Barren geese are easily distinguished by the yellow-green cere which covers most of the bill.*
*FAR RIGHT: Cape Barren geese mate for life, with the female sitting on the eggs and the male protecting the territory. The nests are lined with down.*

beaches and rocky ledges for its habitat. Its food consists of pasture, mainly in the form of grasses. Glands in the bone above the eyes can excrete salt of higher concentration than seawater. Although this mechanism would allow the birds to eat saline ground plants and drink seawater in hard times, their grazing patterns show they prefer freshwater and sweet grasses.

The Cape Barren goose is a strong flier but is not migratory, its major movements being generally from breeding grounds to feeding areas. It is also an able swimmer although it will only enter the water apparently as a last resort — when it is in flightless moult, wounded, or protecting offspring.

Despite being intolerant of their own kind and fiercely territorial during the breeding season, Cape Barren geese are usually found in small groups or flocks. They are believed to pair for life and to return to the same nesting area each season.

The gander helps to build the nest, a pile of vegetation with a shallow, down-lined hollow, on the ground near rocks or tussocks or occasionally above the ground in dense bushes. Between one and seven glossy white eggs are laid, generally in June, and while the female remains on the nest the male defends the territory. The incubation period lasts about five weeks and the offspring, boldly striped in grey and dark brown, leave the nest to graze within hours of hatching.

For about the first six weeks the young remain in their own territory, closely guarded by their parents. Then broods begin to gather into groups and, as they fledge, form even larger flocks up to 200 or so birds which lead a nomadic existence within an island group.

Mutton birds, which have breeding grounds in common with Cape Barren geese, were hunted by Tasmanian Aboriginals during the breeding season. Whether they also hunted Cape Barren geese is not known, but large numbers were certainly killed by sealers operating in Bass Strait in the early 1800s and the population fell sharply. After the 1820s Aboriginals and descendants of the sealers living on the islands continued to hunt the birds for food. Landholders, maintaining that the geese were agricultural pests, also killed them. Goose shooting remained a popular sport until banned in 1959.

Unlike the magpie goose, *Anseranas semipalmata*, once abundant in southern Australia but now confined to the far north coast, the Cape Barren geese have held their own. Numbers were known to be increasing in the 1960s and 1970s, and the Cape Barren goose is now protected by law and several island breeding grounds are reserves.

# Magpie Geese

Related to ducks, swans and true geese in the family Anatidae, magpie geese are placed in a separate sub-family Anseranatinae, of which they are the sole member. They have long, convoluted windpipes, strong bills with a hook on the end and partly webbed toes — they are really quite unmistakable birds.

Magpie geese moult their flight feathers successively so that they are at no time flightless but their weight, sometimes up to three kilograms, can give them some trouble during take-off. To become airborne they crouch low and then leap upward with all their might, their wings flailing before they flap laboriously away.

Once found breeding in colonies along rivers across the north coast and down the east coast of Australia including Victoria and southeastern South Australia, magpie geese *Anseranas semipalmata* are now found only in the coastal rivers of northern

and far northeastern Australia and in southern New Guinea being seen in the southern States only as very rare vagrants.

Their needs are very specialised and their movements on the swamps and river floodplains where they feed and breed are determined by the extent of the wet season each year. Though magpie geese can swim, they seldom do because the swamps that form their refuges are so densely vegetated that the geese get little chance to paddle unhindered. Most of their time they clamber in thick clumps of reed and weed in negotiating their home.

The birds often upend themselves to feed on the succulent bulbous roots of the spike rush, lotus and water lily. They also strain beakfuls of mud from the bottom and will strip seedheads from the grasses to make a meal. When the grasses are too tall, they are flattened under foot to bring the seedheads within reach.

During the height of the dry season, geese resort to digging spike rush bulbs from hard-baked clay with their strong hooked bills. This may be their only source of food for several weeks.

The first flurry of breeding activity begins with the first rains, but nesting does not occur until water levels are suitable. This is generally near the end of the wet season to avoid clutch loss by flooding, but the timing of egg-laying varies according to local conditions in different swamps, or even in different parts of the same swamp. Throughout the wet season, platforms are built by pulling down and trampling grasses.

Magpie geese mate for life and though males may have only one mate, they most often have two. All three share in nest building, incubation and care of the young and both females lay in the same nest. The average is six to eight eggs per nest, though as few as one and as many as sixteen have also been recorded.

Incubation takes 24 or 25 days and is more a matter of standing over the eggs to shade them than of sitting on them to keep them warm. Young are incapable of flight in the first eleven weeks of life and if the swamps dry out too quickly, many will perish.

The family is the basic unit of the social structure, presided over by the dominant male. Flocks are aggregations of different family groups and are made up of different families from one day to the next. A flock flying over has a strong attraction for birds on the ground and they simply join in, flying off to feed or roost. Flying flocks rarely exceed a few hundred in number. Feeding flocks, however, usually number around five thousand and flocks of up to eighty thousand have been seen.

Magpie geese, like true geese, have a loud, resonant honking voice, the pitch being higher in males than in females. A male's call is usually answered immediately by one or more females. The honks may be uttered intermittently or in rapid sequence with several birds joining in the loud refrain.

# Pelicans

Seven different species are recognised, all belonging to the one genus which divides into two, possibly three groups. The Australian pelican, *Pelecanus conspicillatus*, belongs to a group of four large species and is equally at home on fresh or saltwater.

*Bay Picture Library*

*LEFT: The male pied goose has a bony knob on the top of its head, the female's is less distinct.*
*TOP RIGHT: A flock of pelicans, launching into flight, are leaving their feeding grounds in the shallow water.*
*RIGHT: Pelicans are marvellously adapted to the water and appear very ungainly on land.*

Bay Picture Library

Bay Picture Library

The Australian pelicans' main habitats are estuaries, lagoons or large lakes and billabongs. They prefer to fish in the shallow parts and then preen themselves on the sunny mudbanks and islands.

Pelicans, on the whole, are highly adapted for swimming and are ungainly on land. All species are brilliant fliers, capable of long, sustained soaring flights over great distances. They weigh between four and eleven kilograms and the largest ones have wingspans of almost three metres.

Australian pelicans breed in large colonies, roosting on the ground and rarely perching in bushes and trees.

The most essential adaptation for fishing is the bill. This is not used for storage and holding the fish, as some

LEFT: The great crested grebe with a double-horned crest and chestnut frill around its head sits on a nest.
RIGHT: Two little grebes guard their nest. Both parents incubate the nest and feed the young chicks.

parents and run to meet them on their arrival home.

A parent feeding a large chick must expect a rough struggle. The chick's head is pushed down the parental gullet, with the chick fighting and gyrating in an effort to obtain its food.

Young pelicans begin to fly at 60 to 70 days and shortly after that learn to catch their own fish.

# The Grebe

Grebes often swim very low in the water especially if alarmed and when feeding they dive frequently. They paddle most effectively with their feet both on top of, and under the water. They do not have webbed feet like ducks but their long toes have flaps of skin or lobes which convert their feet to broad, efficient paddles.

## The great crested grebe

With its double-horned crest and chestnut frills about its head, the great crested grebe, *Podiceps cristatus* is a striking and spectacular bird with behaviour to match. At just over 40 centimetres it is almost twice the size of the other two Australian species — the hoary-headed, and little grebe.

The great-crested grebe is renowned for its amazing courtship ritual which begins with a "discovery" ceremony during which one bird makes a far-carrying, two note call.

This serves to draw attention to itself and to the fact that it is looking for a mate. Another bird, attracted by the call, partly spreads its wings and face-ruff, looking a little like a cat. The first bird then approaches the other in a shallow underwater "ripple dive" then rises up beyond it. Both birds then shake their heads together then turn away.

The next sequence of this display is described as a "weed trick" and "weed dance" during which the birds dive and bring up weeds which dangle

people believe, but simply for catching it.

All pelicans breed gregariously, in colonies, varying from about 50 birds to tens of thousands. The largest colonies reported in recent years are of the species the great white pelicans of southern Tanzania: up to 40 000 pairs have been sighted.

The pelicans' courtship is usually short and to the point. After mating, two or three eggs are laid without fuss. Both sexes incubate; while one parent is minding the eggs, the other goes fishing. Incubation takes 35 to 37 days.

## Offsprings recognised

Mother would vehemently deny it but independent judges describe the newly-hatched young as plain ugly: naked and pink at first, turning black and grey later before acquiring a coat. After about three weeks they can walk and do so in large groups. Yet each parent recognises and feeds only its own young in these pods.

Parents feed the very young in the usual fashion, without a problem. However, the large chicks reach into the parents' bill and gullet to obtain food. Feathered chicks recognise their

L. Robinson/NPIAW

from their bills. The courting pair then rush together, colliding breast to breast in a type of dance.

They rise almost upright as they stretch their necks to the limit and then dash across the surface of the water in a penguin-like posture, side by side for several metres. This is sometimes repeated as often as ten times. For dedicated bird watchers this ritual is an unforgettable experience.

Its habitat is mostly in the southeast corner of the continent, in the south-west areas of Western Australia and in parts of Tasmania. Unlike the other two species, the great crested grebe is also a widespread bird in Europe, central Asia and the southern half of Africa.

Usually found singly or in pairs, the great crested grebe inhabits still water lakes, sheltered lagoons and streams, brackish estuaries and swamps where it is an expert swimmer and diver. Its diet consists mainly of aquatic animals and plants.

The male and female are similar in appearance — very dark brown above and silky white below. The flanks are mottled dark brown and grey. Their long necks have a black and rufous ruff and a crested head. The eyes are red and the bill is brown above and carmine below.

The great crested grebe is a fast and efficient diver and is able to swim considerable distances underwater. Before flying, the grebe patters along the surface of the water before take-off.

If alarmed the bird utters a guttural note resembling 'hek' and sinks its body beneath the water, leaving only its long neck stretched above.

In a remarkable and total adaptation to an aquatic life, the great crested grebe constructs a floating nest which is usually moored to rushes or the branches of a floating tree. Usually it rests just above the surface and frequently is quite wet. Passing boats are a dangerous threat; the waves they create can easily wash the eggs off the nesting platform.

The great crested grebe constructs a nest of green rushes, reeds and other water plants. Nesting usually takes place from November to January when a clutch of three to seven eggs is laid. The eggs are pale green but soon become stained by the rotting nest material.

Both parents incubate the eggs and both take part in feeding their young. The chicks hatch after about three weeks and are downy sooty brown above with white stripes on the head, neck and back.

Parent birds have the fascinating habit of encouraging their brood to take a ride on their backs. While small, the chicks are particularly vulnerable to fish and other predators and they soon learn to climb onto the back of one parent while the other parent dives to catch food for them.

Periodically there is a changeover of duties. The parent carrying the brood, flaps its wings and the chicks tumble back into water, swim to the other parent and clamber aboard using the parent's foot as a ramp.

## The hoary-headed grebe

The hoary-headed grebe, *Poliocephalus poliocephalus* is a smaller bird that ranges over the entire Australian continent with the exception of Cape York Peninsula. It was once thought to be exclusive to this continent, but has now been observed in New Zealand too.

It is dark grey above and white below and its black head is covered with narrow, white plumes. This grebe is usually silent but a thin, squeaky voice can be heard when the bird tends its young.

The hoary-headed grebe is a renowned sun lover. It sunbathes at every opportunity, keeping its tail towards the sun with its wings folded and tipped upwards. The sunlight passes through these feathers and heats the black skin of the bird's back. The more heat received from the sun, the less needs to be generated metabolically from food.

Hoary-headed and little grebes sunbathe any time the sun is shining and it is interesting to see their posture change when the sun disappears behind a cloud.

## The little grebe

The Australian little grebe, also called dabchick, *Tachybaptus novaehollandiae*, along with other grebes, eats its own feathers and even feeds them to the newly-hatched young.

Some of these feathers form a plug in the outlet from the stomach and presumably prevent sharp, indigestible particles from entering the intestines. For those grebes that feed largely on fish, the feather mass in the stomach probably holds the fishbones until they are regurgitated.

The most vocal of the species, little grebes often give away their presence by their frequent trilling which is sometimes sung as a duet.

No detailed study has been made of this bird and much is yet to be learned by scientists about how Australian grebes, particularly the great crested grebe, compare with their European versions. It is not yet known why, for instance, the roles of both male and female birds are similar and why their spectacular courtship displays do not always lead directly to mating. These and other questions remained to be solved about the mysterious mating habits of grebes.

# THE FOREST DWELLERS

*The spectacular plumage of the birds of paradise and the curious courting habits of the bowerbirds are all part of the life of the forest. Many of the birds who live here are shy and use the forest cover for protection. Others, like the acrobatic friarbirds, advertise their presence high in the treetops with loud, raucous cries. But all are here for the same reason: to feed on the abundance of nectar, flowers and berries that so many of the forest trees yield each year.*

G. Threlfo/Auscape Int.

R. & D. Keller/A.N.T. Photo Library

# Bowerbirds

These birds are regarded by some experts as the peak of avian evolution. This exalted opinion is due to the birds' considerable achievements in architecture and to the tool-using capabilities developed by some species.

These skills are expressed in the male birds' construction of intricate and elaborate bowers in which to perform their courtship displays. Their painstaking and often spectacular decoration of these courts serve as a sexual stimulant to the females, replacing the exaggerated and flamboyant plumage serving that purpose in their colourful relatives, the birds of paradise, allowing a protective colouration to develop instead. Bowerbirds certainly can't rely on their plumage as an attractor; almost all bowerbirds have short, drab feathers.

However, what they lack in colourful appearances, they certainly make up for in their construction ability of bowers.

Bowers take a variety of shapes and forms. All are decorated with objects such as fruit, flowers, leaves, stones, bones, iridescent insect exoskeletons and man-made objects of all sorts including metal, plastic and paper. Leaves and flowers are immediately replaced when they wilt, often daily. Various species show definite colour preferences and will remove items of an objectionable colour which appear in their private palaces.

Each bower is built and owned by an individual male. Some species paint the walls of their bowers using a mixture of saliva and vegetable matter or charcoal and some have invented tools to assist them in this process. The satin bowerbird, for example, uses a wad of plant fibre as a stopper to regulate the flow of 'paint' from its beak as it wipes it onto the bower walls, and the Australian regent bowerbird uses sticks and twigs as brushes with which to apply its wall paint.

All bowers are built of crisscrossed and interwoven sticks, some of which are glued together with a slimy fungus. The majority of the six Australian bowerbirds build avenue-type bowers. The sticks of the avenue walls are carefully inserted into a stick platform, which is raised to varying heights according to species. Some walls are more or less straight, some lean inward, some are distinctly curved and some actually meet at the top to form a tunnel. Avenue walls are painted with various plant pigments.

Decorating tastes are also distinctive. The floor of the platform and the avenue of great bowerbirds is thickly strewn with bleached bones and shells, white stones, flowers, fruits and leaves.

Fawn-breasted bowerbirds favour flowers and fruits, particularly in bunches, with occasional grey-green leaves. Spotted bowerbirds show a penchant for white, using berries, seed pods, shells, bones and stones as well as all sorts of garbage such as paper and broken glass. They also like green glass, but will remove red, blue and yellow objects.

Regent bowerbirds also use shells and pebbles, and have a fancy for shiny black, blue and red objects or fruits, occasionally adding fresh young pinkish leaves. Satin bowerbirds will tolerate green and yellow, but their passion is for blue — so much so that there have been reports of bowerbirds killing small blue birds for their feathers. Flowers and berries are also used and these birds are skilled at acquiring all sorts of blue plastic objects: straws, bottle tops, clothes pegs and bits of paper often adorn their bowers.

The smallest species, golden bowerbirds *Prionodura newtoniana*, build the largest bowers, which differ markedly from those of the other Australian bowerbirds. Selection of site is an important part of this structure as the bird must locate two saplings about a metre apart with a low bridging

TOP: *Decorating his bower with bleached bones and shells and white stones, the great bowerbird is very similar in appearance to the spotted bowerbird.*
ABOVE: *Spotted catbird hatchlings expectantly wait for a meal of insects.*

branch or vine. Conical towers of sticks are built around each tree — usually two or three metres high and not necessarily equal. These towers are decorated with white grey and green lichens and mosses and with white or green fruits and flowers. Scattered about the main bower and the clearing it occupies are often small structures strongly resembling native huts. Displays are performed on the elevated bridge. In this species, unlike in others, females and immature males sometimes help to build the bower and are allowed to play in it, though it is aggressively defended against other adult males. Bowers are constantly maintained during the breeding season, which varies according to species, and sometimes through most of the year. Females visit the bowers and copulation takes place in the bower or nearby.

Bowerbirds have a stunning repertoire of displays, some for courtship

Frithfoto/A.N.T. Photo Library

interior and almost to the west coast.

Those birds living near populated areas are quite bold and have been reported to enter houses to eat crumbs or to steal ornaments for their bowers.

# Birds of Paradise

As the early morning mist rises from Lake Eacham in north Queensland, a harsh cry echoes from the rainforest canopy. It is the first announcement that the riflebird is preparing for another day of courtship rituals. In a few moments he will glide in to his favourite perch, ruffle his feathers with a characteristic sound like paper shuffling and launch into a display matched by few birds.

The Australian riflebirds, of which there are two species, belong to the same family as the New Guinean birds of paradise, Paradisaeidae. Also included in this family are the manucode.

The riflebird inhabits rainforest in northeastern Australia, where it feeds on a variety of foods including fruit, insects, tree frogs and small reptiles. It gained the name of riflebird either because its plumage resembles the fatigues worn by servicemen in the jungle, or because the sheen of its feathers bears a strong resemblance to the sheen of a highly polished rifle.

and some for pure joy. These often involve picking up bright objects from the bower. Some have been observed to give a display when no other birds were in sight. Some displays are performed with extraordinary grace, others with ridiculous clumsiness. All have strong vocal accompaniment, much of it unpleasant to the human ear, and most bowerbirds are accomplished mimics of both animal and mechanical sounds as well as of the calls of other birds.

Male bowerbirds mate with more than one female and, having exercised their inherent nest-building instincts in bower construction, take no part in building nests or rearing young.

Females build cup- or saucer-shaped nests of twigs in the vicinity of the bowers — which themselves seem to occupy circumscribed areas — and lay two or three eggs.

Bowerbirds eat mostly fruits and make a nuisance of themselves in fruit growing districts. They also eat insects which form a large proportion of the diet of nestlings and fledglings.

Though primarily birds of wet tropical habitats, some have adapted to different conditions. The Australian regent bowerbird has moved as far south as the Hawkesbury estuary and the satin bowerbird all the way to southern coastal Victoria. The spotted bowerbird has moved into the arid

F. Park/A.N.T. Photo Library

D. V. Matthews/A.N.T. Photo Library

*TOP: Sporting distinct 'serrations' on its bill, the toothbilled catbird is found in northeastern Queensland.*

*LEFT: A male spotted bowerbird with a distinctive lilac patch on his head.*

*ABOVE: This young male satin bowerbird adds blue objects to a bower which may not necessarily be his.*

Both our species of riflebird share similar characteristics and habits, but their range does not overlap. The magnificent riflebird has a very limited range, extending from Cape York to the Chester River in Queensland. The paradise riflebird covers a much larger area, from Mackay to the Hunter River in New South Wales.

Neither species seems to be in danger of extinction but loss of habitat has, as with many rainforest species, reduced their numbers considerably.

Like the bowerbird, the male riflebird has a well defined display area, usually a thick horizontal branch 5 metres or more from the ground. There he spends much of his time during the breeding season, calling and displaying.

He spreads his wings, swaying from side to side, before swinging upside down from the branch, all the time emitting a harsh shriek. When the female arrives on the scene the male becomes increasingly agitated. He dances about her, sometimes backwards, and claps his wings against hers.

After mating the male has little to do with the female. He is free to mate again with another partner should his display prove successful, while the female builds the nest and raises the young alone. This unequal division of labour is fairly common among birds with marked plumage differences between the sexes — a brightly coloured male is not particularly well camouflaged for domestic duties.

This difference between the sexes is even more pronounced among New Guinean birds of paradise, where the males are without doubt the most brilliantly coloured in the world. These beautiful creatures first became known when some skins arrived in the Spanish court in 1522. Only the rugged mountains of the Highlands saved them from extinction, as demand for their feathers quickly outstripped supply.

Many myths surrounded the birds of paradise and persisted until well into the nineteenth century. As the skins taken back to Europe had the legs removed, many people believed that the birds spent all their life in the air, feeding on the dew of heaven. The female supposedly laid her egg in a hollow in the male's back where it was incubated and hatched.

Fortunately, today birds of paradise

Bay Picture Library

are protected in New Guinea, except when taken for use in tribal customs. But, like the riflebird, they need strict monitoring to ensure their survival.

*ABOVE: Plumage from the greater bird of paradise, as with other birds of paradise is still used in New Guinean's tribal customs. The Australian riflebird belongs to the New Guinea birds of paradise family.*

# The Sunbird

The sunbird probably derives its name from its colouring. From below, the sight of its bright yellow underparts is like a flash of sunlight. It belongs to one of the families of nectar-sippers, Nectariniidae. Another family of nectar-sippers is the Trochilidae, the family of the American hummingbird.

The sunbird and the hummingbird are both diminutive, very beautiful, and with specialized flight techniques. But it must be admitted that in all respects the hummingbird is the bird 'with the mostest'. The sunbird is beautiful but the hummingbird is gorgeous; and the flight technique of the hummingbird is superior since, in

proportion to its size, it uses far more wing beats (up to 60 per second) than the other species. Normally, the rate of wing beat increases in inverse proportion to the size of a bird, and the fewer the wing beats, the greater the flight efficiency.

The Australian species of sunbird, *Nectarinia jugularis*, usually dwells on the edge of rain forests. Except in the breeding period it is solitary and sedentary. Both males and females measure about 12 centimetres.

Though slightly built, the sunbird has powerful feet which allow it to hold onto twigs and plants. Mostly arboreal, it feeds on flowering trees, only occasionally exploiting flowers lower down. It has a long thin

downward-curving bill; and a tube-like tongue with which it can suck nectar from flowers and, when it fancies, extract spiders and insects from the flowers. It does this while hovering or, sometimes, while clinging to foliage. Spiders and insects are, in fact, an essential part of its diet.

The male is more brightly coloured than the female. Its underparts are yellow and its upper body a yellowish green with iridescent patches on the chin and upper breast. In the non-breeding season, however, its colouring may become more drab. In the female, the throat and breast are yellow as well as the underparts.

The breeding period is from August to March. The female is the caring parent: she builds the nest, the male sitting by and supervising her efforts; she lays two or three eggs; she does most of the incubating; and she feeds the chicks until they are about a week old. But she cannot protect her offspring from the butcherbird which often preys on the same sunbird family through many broods.

The nest is made from bark and foliage, all bound together with cobwebs. Some nests boast a type of side entrance near the top. The whole structure is suspended from the branches of low trees or, when the birds are living in association with man, from clothes lines or the edge of verandahs or windows. Sunbirds are not enthusiastic builders. Often, they make do with the same nest for years, carrying out running repairs only when necessary.

# Cuckoo-Shrikes

Their only connection with cuckoos and shrikes is that they belong to the same order, the Passeriformes, the order of perching birds. This is a very tenuous connection since more than half of all the birds in the world are perching birds.

Cuckoo-shrikes are members of the family Campephagidae, a word which

*LEFT: The male magnificent riflebird has glossy dark feathers and brilliant blue feathers around the throat. In comparison, the female has a drab brown and grey colouring; beneficial as camouflage when nesting.*

means 'caterpillar-eater'. The family is represented in Africa as well as in Australia, New Guinea and other islands of the Pacific.

In the southern hemisphere (excluding the African continent) there are seven species, five of them belonging to the genus *Coracina*, and the others, known as trillers, to the genus *Lalage*. They are medium sized birds, length ranging from 18 centimetres to 36 centimetres. Their colouring is subdued — usually grey with black and white markings. This is indicated by one of their common names 'greybird'. Their lower back is covered with loosely-attached feathers, a feature which frustrates predators who are often left with a few feathers in the beak and no bird in the claws.

Another of their common names is 'shufflewing'. When settling on a branch they fold and unfold their wings, a type of display behaviour which is puzzling even to ornithologists.

Most members of the family are forest-dwelling, with two exceptions, one species being a tree-dweller and the other, the ground cuckoo-shrike, living in open country. Their lifestyle is migratory, migrations being governed by season and the availability of food. The food items which cuckoo-shrikes fancy most are insects, fruit and berries.

The breeding season is from August to December. During this period they lay two to three eggs which are bluish in colour with dark blotches. The nest is usually shaded but situated precariously on the outer edge of a branch. It is also fragile, and so small and shallow that the fledglings often tumble out and onto the ground.

## The black-faced cuckoo

The most common species is the black-faced cuckoo-shrike, *Coracina novae-hollandiae*. This bird ranges over most of Australia, New Guinea and other islands of the Pacific. It is also known as 'blue jay' and 'blue pigeon' and, in Tasmania, as 'summerbird'. It is about 33 centimetres long. Colour is a bluish grey on the body and black on the head, the black colour being outlined in such a way as to give the bird the appearance of wearing a mask. In flight, it emits a series of pleasing rolling notes.

## The ground cuckoo-shrike

The ground cuckoo-shrike, *C. maxima*, ranges through the inland areas of Australia. It is approximately 36 centimetres long, the largest member of the family and the only one to adapt to feeding on the ground. While it seeks its food on the ground, it builds its nest in trees, usually at a great height. Two females of the species may lay their eggs in the same nest, which is most unusual behaviour for birds.

## The cicada bird

The cicada bird, *C. tenuirostris*, so called because of the nature of its call, is much smaller, about 27 centimetres long. It is not often seen, as it seeks shelter high up in trees. Both male and female build the nest; the female sits in it; and is fed by the male. When the young are born both parents cooperate in feeding them. In Australia the cicada bird ranges from Broome in the northwest, along the north coast of the continent, and southward as far as Melbourne.

## The yellow-eyed and white-breasted cuckoo-shrike

The yellow-eyed cuckoo-shrike, *C. lineata*, is about 29 centimetres long. In Australia it ranges through rainforests on the northeast coast of the continent. The species uses a communal roost, a sociable attitude which it does not carry into the breeding period.

Some ornithologists consider that there are two variations in Australia: within the species *C. papuensis*, the white-breasted bird of northern Australia, and the grey-breasted form which ranges northward along the eastern coast from Townsville to Cape York Peninsula. The common name of *C. papuensis* is white-bellied cuckoo-shrike.

## Trillers

Trillers, the smallest of the cuckoo-shrikes, belong to a separate genus, *Lalage*. Their common name derives from their tremulous vibrating calls.

There are two species, the white-winged triller, *Lalage sueurii*, and the

*ABOVE: A Victoria male riflebird displays on a perch to attract mates. Part of this display includes the riflebird stretching his wings in a fan around the body and opening his mouth to display the brightly coloured inner lining.*

varied triller, *L. leucomela*. Both species are about 18 centimetres long and, at first glance, it would be easy to mistake one for the other were it not for the distinctive white eyebrow of *L. leucomela*.

As is the case with animals of other orders, the male *L. sueurii* is much more beautiful than the female. It is strikingly marked in black and white, while the female is drab and unobtrusive. The species is unusual in that it moults twice a year. After moulting the male becomes as drab as the female.

# Pittas

Pittas, or dragoon-birds as they are sometimes called, are stout and sturdy, about 170–190 millimetres in length. Being ground-dwelling birds, their legs are well developed and quite muscular. The three species found in Australia are characterised by the bright colours and short tails.

## The noisy pitta

The best known of the pittas is the noisy pitta, *Pitta versicolor*, found along the east coast from the Central Coast

*ABOVE: A male sunbird at its nest which consists of bark and foliage bound together by spider webs and suspended from low-hanging tree branches.*
*ABOVE RIGHT: Sunbirds have long curved bills which enable them to successfully search for nectar, spiders and insects in flowers. This is a female sunbird.*

of New South Wales to Cape York. The head and neck are black, except for a chestnut 'skull cap'.

The rest of the body is strikingly coloured: the back is bright green, with iridescent turquoise on the shoulder; the belly and chest is buff or yellow; the vent region is red and the flight feathers, not often observed, are black.

Despite its shy nature, the noisy pitta is thought to be fairly common, for its presence can be easily detected from a number of tell-tale signs.

Because of the dense rainforest in which they are, members of a group must keep in contact by means other than sight. Thus, there is an almost continuous calling between individuals, especially during the breeding season.

The call of the noisy pitta, according to Neville Cayley, rhymes with,

'want a watch' or 'walk to work', usually repeated twice. At night it also utters long, mournful notes.

Another sign of the pitta's presence is the small 'middens' it leaves. Basically insectivorous, but also fond of berries and fruit, the noisy pitta has developed a unique way of extracting land snails from their shells.

It uses a stone or tree stump as an anvil, against which it strikes the snail shell. When the shell is finally cracked, the soft internal flesh is eaten and the cracked shell discarded.

Favoured 'anvils' invariably have a small pile of snail shells at their base. Some birds make such frequent use of their 'anvils' that they become quite smooth from the constant pounding.

The breeding season for noisy pittas is usually from October to January. A dome-shaped nest with a side entrance is built, composed of twigs, moss, strips of bark and roots, sometimes secured by the addition of mud.

The interior is lined with decaying wood, possibly as a means of providing a material to absorb the faeces of the young. The nest is usually placed at the base of a large tree, often amongst large buttress roots.

One peculiar feature of the noisy pitta's nest is the use of animal dung

as a 'doormat'. Mammal dung in particular is preferred, but for what reason is not clear. Perhaps it acts as a discouragement to potential predators who, sensing that they may be in another predator's territory, depart before investigating the nest.

Noisy pittas have a complex migratory pattern that is yet to be fully studied. It seems that the entire population moves north in winter, birds from southern regions moving into Queensland, and birds from further north flying to New Guinea and nearby islands.

Some birds, however, seem to remain in their area all year while others, such as those on the Atherton Tableland, move into lowland areas.

## The rainbow pitta

Closely allied to the noisy pitta is the rainbow pitta, *P. iris*. Both birds share many habits as far as is known, but the rainbow pitta is even more elusive and has not been studied closely.

The rainbow pitta is found in the far north of Australia, along the 'top end' west from the Gulf of Carpentaria. Unlike the noisy pitta, it is not confined to rainforest, but has also colonised mangroves, bamboo thickets and forested river margins.

The rainbow pitta is slightly smaller than the noisy pitta, and in markings differs somewhat. The head, neck and belly are black, with chestnut stripes on the head. The vent region is red, but covers a smaller area than in the noisy pitta. The back is green and the iridescent turquoise area is larger.

The rainbow pitta spends most of its time on the ground, warily searching for worms, insects and snails. Its call is similar to that of the noisy pitta. Just how common it is has not been ascertained, but it does appear to be uncommon.

The nest of the rainbow pitta varies according to locality; in the Kimberleys it may be an insubstantial open structure placed in a tussock of grass; in other areas it tends to be the typical pitta dome-shaped nest, placed about two metres above the ground in a clump of bamboo or a stand of mangroves. There is no use made of animal dung according to the limited number of reports.

The rainbow pitta appears to be the only Australian pitta that has taken up residence; the other two species are migratory birds although the noisy pitta is not migratory across the entire range.

## The red-bellied pitta

The red-bellied pitta, *P. erythrogaster*, is seen on Cape York during the wet season, when it appears for breeding. The rest of its time is spent in New Guinea.

*BELOW: Sitting on a shallow nest built into the fork of a tree, this adult white-bellied cuckoo-shrike incubates the eggs.*

*ABOVE: The cicada bird which shelters high up in trees is a member of the cuckoo-shrike family.*

*ABOVE RIGHT: Smallest of the cuckoo-shrikes, this male varied triller tends the nest, which is also built in the fork of a tree branch.*

The red-bellied pitta is a particularly attractive bird, but is highly secretive. Its markings vary significantly between the 26 recorded races found in Micronesia and Melanesia.

Basically, the red-bellied pitta can be recognised by its blue-green back, blue wings, tail, rump and upper chest, red belly and the brick-red colour at the back of the head.

The call of the red-bellied pitta is often uttered from a tall tree, fifteen metres or more above the ground, and is a mournful combination of four notes, occasionally with a rasping edge.

Though rarely seen, the red-bellied pitta may be observed hopping across the forest floor in search of insects. It has a characteristic motion, involving jerking of the head and flicking the tail that may be a means of flushing insects from the leaf litter.

The red-bellied pitta's nest is dome-shaped, composed of twigs and leaves and lined with fine fibres, placed on a stump or in a tangle of vines one to three metres above the ground. Three to four creamy-white eggs are laid, but incubation details, as in the other species of Australian pittas, are not known.

# Friarbirds

Friarbirds are among the largest members of that well known family of birds, the honeyeaters. There are four species of friarbirds in Australia and each has the typical honeyeater feature of a long, tapering down-curved bill, designed for inserting into flowers to obtain nectar. They are generally a grey to light brown colour with the most distinguishing feature being their featherless, black head.

John Gould reported that the early settlers named these birds 'friar' or 'monk' birds, no doubt in recognition of the similarities with certain members of the religious fraternity! The other characteristic feature of all species, except the little friarbird, is a small knob or helmet on the top of the upper bill. The purpose of this knob may be a sign of maturity and of specific identification, as it is poorly developed in immature birds.

The little friarbird also differs from the others by the blue tinge on its face and the immature birds having a yellow throat. When John Gould first described this species in 1836 he chose the specific name *citreogularis*, referring to the yellow throat. However, he later realised that the specimen he had used was an immature bird. Despite this slight error the name has remained the same.

The four species are restricted to the eastern and northern parts of the Australian mainland, with two also living in New Guinea and nearby islands. Friarbirds do not occur in Tasmania.

The silver-crowned friarbird, *Philemon argenticeps*, is found across northern Australia, extending from the Kimberleys through to Cape York Peninsula. The helmeted friarbird, *P. buceroides*, lives on the Queensland coast from Mackay to Cape York. It also occurs in the top part of the Northern Territory, New Guinea, Torres Strait islands and Timor. The noisy friarbird, *P. corniculatus*, occurs through most of the eastern part of Queensland, New South Wales and into Victoria. The most widespread species is the smaller little friarbird, *P. citreogularis*, which has a similar range to the noisy friarbird, but extending through to the Kimberleys.

Generally the four species inhabit wet and dry forest and woodland, congregating in areas where trees are flowering. The helmeted and silver-crowned tend to be nomadic, moving to areas where the trees are blossoming. Melaleuca swamps and mangroves are particularly popular. The noisy friarbird tends to have a distinct migratory pattern in the south of its range. They usually arrive in large numbers in September and then retreat in a northerly direction to Queensland in April and May.

When friarbirds gather in a tree that is heavy in blossom, there is much squabbling between individuals of the same and other species. In the excitement, the birds will perform many acrobatic twists and turns to reach the flowers. It is not uncommon to see them hanging by one leg as they poke their bill into the flowers.

The helmeted friarbird found an unusual source of food in the canefields of Queensland many years ago. They would gather in large numbers and feed on the juice of the sugar cane that had been burnt and left in the field for several days. Today this no longer

*TOP LEFT: A noisy pitta provides a meal of juicy earthworms for its young chicks.*
*LEFT: Unlike its relatives, the rainbow pitta is thought to be non-migratory. Its range (distribution) is much more restrictive than the less-adaptable noisy pitta. The rainbow pitta is found in the NT.*

Graeme Chapman/Auscape Int.

Jean-Paul Ferrero/Auscape Int.

occurs, as the cane is collected very soon after burning.

Nectar is not the only food source for friarbirds. Insects are also important. They will catch larger insects on the wing, such as the Christmas beetles which are very abundant in December and January. In Canberra, the Argyle apple eucalypt, *Eucalyptus cinerea*, is a common street tree. These support a large number of insects which feed on the leaves and flowers. The insects are in turn eagerly sought by many birds, including the noisy friarbird. Up to twenty friarbirds have been seen feeding in three of these trees for up to an hour before moving on. They were busily plucking small scale insects, caterpillars and beetles from the foliage.

Such voracious feeding highlights the value of these and other birds as natural agents for controlling pests, thus reducing the need to use chemicals. Many of the street trees in Canberra used to be sprayed to kill the

*ABOVE LEFT: A noisy friarbird feasts on some Lawthorn berries. Its diet also includes voraciously sought insects.*
*ABOVE RIGHT: Acrobatically feeding, the helmeted friarbird, along with the other members of its family, is a pest in orchards.*

---

insects. This action often killed many birds such as the friarbirds. Fortunately this spraying has virtually ceased, leaving the control of insects to birds and other predatory animals.

While friarbirds help control insect pests, they themselves can become pests in orchards. As a result, they have been shot in large numbers in past years. Today they are protected throughout most of their range.

As well as being shot as pests, some species were shot as game birds. This took place on the north coast of New South Wales, where the noisy friarbird, along with other large honeyeaters, were shot mainly to test the skill of the shooter. The 'sport' ceased in 1945.

Breeding time for all species is usually September to April. While friarbirds are gregarious birds when feeding, they pair off and generally become shy and retiring when breeding. They build a bulky cup nest using strips of bark, wool, grass, leaves and spiderweb. The nest is usually located in the outer foliage of branches at a height ranging from two to fifteen metres above the ground. The female incubates the eggs herself, with the male remaining nearby. Once the young have hatched, both parents help feed the young.

Friarbirds have a particular liking for water and can be often seen bathing in pools of water. The helmeted friarbird is known to bath in the pools and spray at the base of waterfalls.

Despite some species being shot in the past, all species remain abundant in their range. And with more native plants being established in cities and towns they should continue to be regular visitors to the urban gardens.

# BIRDS OF THE HIGH SEAS

*There are many ocean-going birds around Australia's coastline and islands which nest in huge, noisy colonies away from human habitation. Much of their life is spent on the wing.*

*A seabird has many adaptations for life at sea, not the least of which is its ability to drink saltwater. Whereas the Ancient Mariner was confronted with 'water, water everywhere, but not a drop to drink', seabirds can drink saltwater freely and rid themselves of the excess salt. This is done through nostrils, often giving the impression that they are blowing their noses sans handkerchiefs.*

## Albatrosses

Albatrosses are closely related to fulmars, petrels, prions and shearwaters, all of which spend most of their time in flight. Known as tube-nosed seabirds (order Procellariiformes) they all have long tubular nostrils opening out of the hooked bill. These are exposed in some species but are less obvious in albatrosses, which although still exposed are covered by horny plates. Some ornithologists believe the tubular structure may give these birds a heightened sense of smell.

Albatrosses eating habits vary. Many species, including the wandering albatross, follow ships and boats to gather food from waste thrown overboard or from trailing nets. They also feed on cuttlefish, squid, crustaceans, food discarded by other predators and on dead dolphin and whale. They may seize food from the surface while in flight but often sit on the water to feed — a risky business as the birds cannot take flight again unless the wind is strong. Sometimes a bird renders itself incapable of taking off if it has overeaten and will regurgitate food to lessen its weight and make flight easier.

In spite of their reputation as an omen of good luck and the seaman's friend, immortalised in Samuel Taylor Coleridge's *The Rime of the Ancient Mariner*, albatrosses were often killed for their meat and their breeding

*ABOVE: The heavy-bodied wandering albatross guards over its chick. The egg would have taken up to 75 days to hatch and three days for the chick to break out of its shell.*

M. F. Soper/A.N.T. Photo Library

grounds raided for eggs by hungry sailors and sealers. Several north Pacific species were hunted for their plumage in the nineteenth century and some lost their nesting grounds as European settlement expanded.

### The wandering albatross

Also known as the cape sheep, the wandering albatross, *Diomedea exulans*, is one of about 14 species of albatross found mainly in the southern oceans between latitudes 30°S and 60°S. They

are heavy-bodied birds with short legs, but their long, narrow wings with spans from 3.5 to 4 metres allow them to soar effortlessly for days on end. Some individuals may circumnavigate the world twice a year in the westerly winds of the 'roaring forties'.

The wandering albatross mates for life after an elaborate courtship ritual of bowing, dancing and bill clapping. Unless a chick is lost, most pairs mate every second year, the breeding cycle beginning in September. Pairs return to the same nesting site in colonies on remote subantarctic islands such as Macquarie Island, and build a cone-shaped nest of earth and grass.

Only one large egg, white speckled with reddish brown, is laid. It takes up to 75 days to hatch — one of the longest of all bird incubations — and

R. Thonkins/A.N.T. Photo Library

Bay Picture Library

P. J. Fullager/Auscape Int.

*ABOVE: With a wingspan a little less than two and a half metres long, the black-browed albatross is one of the smaller albatrosses.*
*ABOVE RIGHT: Muttonbirds, harvested each year for their meat, are known to live up to at least 36 years.*
*RIGHT: Found only on Norfolk and Lord Howe Islands, the providence petrel migrates to other Pacific regions.*

the chick takes three days to break out of the shell. For the next eight months or so both parents tend the chick, feeding it on regurgitated, partly digested food. When a parent returns for feeding, it greets the chick with effusive bowing, followed by a pulsating braying call. The tail is fanned, the head, neck and bill are angled sharply downward and the cheek patches pulled back exposing a strip of bright orange skin under the eye; the head and neck are moved up and down while the bill is clattered.

Oddly, this same display is used when another adult intrudes into the bird's territory. If the bowing display is ignored the gaping display is performed, the bird standing upright with tail fanned, neck stretched and bill wide open. The head is jerked from side to side, the wings are raised threateningly and the call given again, louder. In an actual confrontation, billing displays are performed. Combat is ritualised and the defeated bird retreats with body hunched and neck withdrawn. The birds seem to know

the outcome of the contest before it begins and actual fighting is extremely rare.

Chicks also have aggressive displays. If rapid bill clapping goes unheeded, a stream of oily, foul-smelling, partly digested food is ejected, delivered with uncanny accuracy over a distance of up to 2 metres. The chicks have dark bills and are covered with fluffy white down. They leave the nest in spring when fully

fledged, but take ten years to attain adult plumage. A mature bird, which may live for 35–40 years, has white plumage with brown scalloping down its wings which are edged in black, as are the white underwings. The eyes are brown and the curved, pale pink bill has a rounded tip. It is very similar to the royal albatross, *D. epomorpha*, which is a rare visitor in Australian waters but nests in New Zealand and its associated islands.

*ABOVE: Not a common species of gadfly petrels, the Kermadec petrel has a colony on a rocky outcrop known as Ball's Pyramid which is some distance from Lord Howe Island. The Kermadec petrel may have either dark or light plumage.*

Getting to and from the nesting grounds is often a complicated business for the wandering albatross. The wings have a high stall speed which makes accurate landing difficult except into a strong wind. On still days, the approach is often misjudged and the birds may pull away at the last moment to try again or land in an extremely awkward and undignified manner, bowling over neighbours and causing havoc as aggressive displays are mounted from whole sections of the colony. If a wind is blowing, the birds drop into it with wings highly angled, tail fanned downward and webbed feet spread like the flaps and brakes of an aeroplane.

They sometimes aim for high, unoccupied ground then walk down through the crowded rookery to their nests, but must tolerate the territorial aggression of both adults and chicks they pass. The same thing happens when they want to take off on still days and must walk through the rookery to launch themselves into flight over a cliff edge. On windy days, however, takeoff is effortless. The bird simply stands on a rock and, spreading the wings, is lifted and carried away by the wind.

The wandering albatross has few natural enemies and, unlike some more northerly species, has suffered little at the hands of man.

The only albatross to breed in Australia is the white-capped albatross, *Diomedea canta*, which is the largest of the 'mollymawks', an alternative name for some smaller albatrosses. It nests on Albatross Rock in Bass Strait, on offshore Pedra Branca south of Tasmania and also breeds on Mewstone.

## Superstition on the wing

Old sailors used to firmly believe that killing an albatross brought bad luck to their ship. Of course, many a ship met with disaster even in the ordinary course of events — so nobody will ever know what part, if any, albatrosses played in sea mayhems.

It's impossible to trace the origin of this superstition — or even the grounds for it. Sydney scientist Graeme Phipps says that as albatrosses are very cosmopolitan, occurring in just about every ocean, the superstition might have started in any of dozens of seafaring countries.

"One theory I have heard," he says, "is that sailors believed albatrosses housed the spirit of dead seamen who then took revenge for the slaughter of the birds. But who knows, really, what they believed in?"

Why should anyone kill an albatross? Their meat is tough to eat and

not particularly tasty. Then, smart sailors would have usually greeted the presence of these birds with some joy as they indicated the proximity of some land — or at least served as navigational aids.

# Muttonbirds

Like the albatrosses, the muttonbirds which, as a general term, also include flesh-footed, wedge-tailed, sooty and short-tailed shearwaters, have been hunted by man for meat and other products. However, unlike albatrosses, the hunting continues today, by as many as 70 000 a year. On Tasmania's rugged coast and the windswept Furneaux Islands off the Bass Strait for five weeks of each year, young shearwaters are pulled from

their burrows, their necks broken and threaded onto poles.

The short-tailed shearwater lives an amazing, if not precarious life. Breeding only in Australia, they make their burrows under grass tussocks, and each mature female lays only one egg in a nest at the end of the burrow. The parent birds, which are dark brown and about the size of our familiar silver gulls, feed the chicks on regurgitated food until they are three months old (the adult birds feed at sea, taking whatever floats on the surface, and also diving for fish. Local abalone divers have seen the muttonbirds swimming underwater at depths of 10 metres.)

If the chicks survive this long, they will have avoided the first danger — that of being harvested — only to be confronted with the equally daunting prospect of a migratory flight of more than 30 000 kilometres.

*ABOVE: Seen here at the entrance of its burrow, the black-winged petrel is around 30 centimetres in length, has dark upperwings, and a pronounced dark edge around the white underwing.*

Spending six to seven months on the wing, they migrate over this enormous distance by riding the prevailing winds, which carry them as far away as Russia and Alaska, and return them across the Pacific Ocean to Australia. The young birds remain at sea, while the mature adults of four years or older land to breed.

Research and surveys are needed to determine the effects of harvesting on the bird population. As yet the guidelines for harvesting are not based on any current research, and do not take into account depletion of bird numbers through loss of suitable habitat (by the extension of grazing land) or through natural hazards (fire,

insufficient food, storms, for example).

As the average life span of the bird is quite long, (some individual birds have lived up to 36 years), a heavily harvested season may not be noticed for 20 years. Clearly, if muttonbirding is to survive at all, we need to have stricter controls and a long-term policy for the conservation of the species.

What is taken for granted as being Australia's most abundant sea bird, may in time become less common, without adequate planning.

# Gadfly Petrels

One of the smaller and most appealing groups of seabirds is the gadfly petrels. This is a rather hazily distinguished group, and opinions vary as to the number of species that should be included. For the most part, twenty to thirty species are recognised. Of these, eleven have been identified in Australian waters, but only seven can be called locals.

Gadfly petrels, all of which fall into the genus *Pterodroma*, closely resemble the more familiar shearwaters, but can often be quickly distinguished. When in flight the species are easily separated. The gadflys have shorter bills, and the nasal tube, prominent in many seabirds, is tilted slightly upwards. The wings of petrels are often broader, and their tails longer. All range between 25 and 40 centimetres in length, and are found in tropical and subtropical waters.

settlement. Food was running desperately low, so the few food resources on Norfolk were exploited to the limit. The providence petrel was in abundance on Mt Pitt, and having no knowledge of man, was easily caught.

As a result of this harvesting the providence petrel is rarely seen on Norfolk Island but on Lord Howe Island there is still a good sized breeding population of some 20 000 pairs.

The birds arrive in March and begin circling high over the mountains at the southern end of the island. Most

*LEFT: This pied cormorant outstretched drying its feathers is a common sight. Cormorant's feathers, unlike most other aquatic birds, are not waterproof.*
*BELOW: Truly oceanic birds, black-faced cormorants will congregate during the breeding season in large numbers on rocky offshore islands and platforms.*

before this. Many seem to migrate to other parts of the Pacific after breeding, with birds recorded as far afield as Japan and Hawaii.

Programmes carried out on Lord Howe to preserve woodhen habitat from destruction from pigs and cats should ensure the survival of the providence petrel. Plans are also afoot to reconstruct a breeding colony on Norfolk Island by hatching a large number of eggs there and hand-raising the chicks. If this is successful, it would be a great feat by the National Parks and Wildlife Service. With only one breeding colony, there is always the chance of minor environmental changes wiping out the entire population.

## The Kermadec petrel

Another gadfly petrel found on Lord Howe is the Kermadec petrel, *P.*

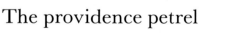

H. & J. Beste/NPIAW

## The providence petrel

The providence petrel, *P. solandri*, was one of the first species in Australian waters to come to the attention of the early colonists. It was extremely common on Norfolk Island up until the early 1800s. The last three years have seen its return to Norfolk Island. It is also found on Lord Howe Island.

The reason for its rapid decline on Norfolk Island was excessive hunting by the starving inhabitants of the penal

petrels come in to land at dusk but the providence petrels begin landing around midday, continuing through the afternoon with a loud and raucous display.

The sight of thousands of these birds darting through the mist and salt spray that cloaks the mountains is a spectacular sight indeed. Diving and wheeling is the order of the day as they chase one another.

Females lay a single white egg in May or June in a burrow about 60 centimetres long. By November most of the chicks have fledged, but the adults leave the island a few weeks

*neglecta.* The Kermadec petrel is not a common species, and only maintains a small colony on Ball's Pyramid, a rocky outcrop some distance from the main island of Lord Howe. It is rarely seen west of Lord Howe, but is found in several other Pacific areas, including the Kermadec Islands from which it takes its name.

## The black-winged petrel

For many years the position of the black-winged petrel, *P. nigripennis*, was thought to be similar to that of the

*RIGHT: An osprey coming in for landing with a fish firmly grasped in its talons. Osprey pairs use the same nest year after year, continually adding to its structure.*
*BELOW: Osprey chick's tentative first attempts at flying. When they are around two months old, the chicks will make their first flight, accompanying their parents to a fish feeding ground. The chicks then increase their hunting skills, with their parents occasionally helping them out with the odd fish or two. Ospreys feed mainly on live fish.*

H. & J. Beste/Auscape Int.

providence petrel. It had always been considered a rare bird, with only one known breeding site, on the Kermadec Islands, north of New Zealand. That picture seems to be changing.

Since the late 1960s it has expanded its range, and is now found over much of the South Pacific. Breeding sites have been located on Lord Howe, Norfolk and other islands. Several groups have also been sighted along eastern Australian beaches, suggesting they may be seeking potential nesting sites along the coast.

## Gould's petrel

Gould's petrel, *P. leucoptera*, is a species with a particularly restricted breeding range. The smallest of the gadfly petrels, along with the black-winged petrel, it is just 30 centimetres long and breeds only on Cabbage Tree Island at the entrance to Port Stephens, New South Wales. The entire world breeding population of some 500 pairs converges on this 20 hectare island each October and remains there until the following April.

Unlike most other gadfly petrels, Gould's petrel is not reliant on burrows to nest in. It is satisfied with a pile of rocks or a hollow log — in fact anything that offers a minimum of shelter. One white egg is laid, with the majority of these hatching in January. The young are fledged by April.

With such a small population confined to one area for several months of each year, Gould's petrel is clearly a vulnerable species requiring the strictest conservation measures. At present it is fairly secure, with no significant losses on Cabbage Tree Island; but if exotic predators, such as cats or rats become entrenched on the island, the results could be devastating.

M. & I. Morcombe

## The great-winged and white-headed petrel

The position for the other Australian petrels is much more secure, as they generally have several breeding colonies. The great-winged petrel, *P. macroptera*, is one species with a large population, and several nesting sites on islands along the southern and south-western coasts. It is a common bird, often sighted far out to sea, where it feeds on plankton, squid, crustaceans and some fish. Most of their fishing seems to be done at night, when they fly low above the water, skimming the surface and occasionally diving.

The white-headed petrel, *P. lessonii*, is a wide ranging species often seen in southern waters, except along the coast of the Bight. It extends north to midway between Brisbane and Sydney and, in the west, just past the Tropic.

Distinguished by its dark eye patches and white head, this petrel is also found frequenting subantarctic waters, and moves as far south as the Antarctic pack ice in favourable seasons.

## The soft-plumaged petrel

One species of petrel that appears rather sedentary, in sharp contrast to the other species, is the soft-plumaged petrel, *P. mollis*. Predominantly a bird of subantarctic and Indian Ocean waters, it has known colonies on Tristan da Cunha and Gough Islands in the South Atlantic, and Marion and Kerguelen Islands in the Indian Ocean. There is also a strong possibility that it also breeds on the Antipodes Islands in the South Pacific.

The soft-plumaged petrel can be found on these islands for all but a few months of the year. They use the islands as a base, and spread out in their search for food. Sometimes their travels may last only a day or so, sometimes well over a week. In common with many seabirds, they have learnt that by following ships they are likely to pick up a free feed of food scraps from the galley.

# Cormorants

In China and Japan the cormorant is an important part of the tourist trade, being used by fishermen to demonstrate the ancient art of catching fish with a tame bird. Australian fishermen take a somewhat different view, seeing the cormorant as a direct threat to their livelihood.

Australia has five species of cormorant, but only the pied and black-faced species are truly oceanic birds, frequenting beaches, reefs and offshore islands. The black, little black and little pied species prefer estuaries, lakes and inland rivers.

All are fish eaters, but only the black cormorant takes significant quantities of commercially valuable fish. Other aquatic species such as amphibians and crustaceans also form part of the cormorant's diet.

All cormorants are expert divers. Under water they are accomplished swimmers, and can remain submerged for up to 30 seconds. The cormorant's body is perfectly adapted for diving — sleek and streamlined, with the feet set well back along the body. Even a feature which might seem to be a disadvantage is put to good use by the cormorant.

Unlike most other aquatic birds, the cormorant's feathers are not waterproof, but gradually become wet with immersion. This is why it is often seen perched with its wings outstretched, 'hanging its clothes out to dry'.

The absence of waterproof feathers actually improves its diving ability. If the feathers resisted wetting, they would also retain air under water. The wetting of the feathers increases the

Frithfoto/A.N.T. Photo Library

density of the bird under water, making it a much more efficient swimmer.

Other diving birds solve this problem in different ways. Gannets dive from great heights and use this propulsion to give them speed under water. But they cannot swim under water for long periods as the cormorant can.

The cormorant has one further peculiarity that may assist in diving: it swallows pebbles. These are possibly used as ballast to increase the bird's weight and also as grit to aid the breaking up of food in the gizzard.

Marine cormorants are colony breeders, and will congregate in large numbers in the breeding season. On rocky offshore islands and platforms they will group in many thousands.

*LEFT: The Brahminy kite with its chestnut red and white plumage is one of the most attractive birds of prey. It is found along the northern Australian coastline.*
*BELOW: A display of its red pouch is the male frigatebird's distinctive courting ritual.*

Courtship can be a raucous affair, with the male doing much of the calling. It is largely up to the female to decide which mate she prefers.

Marine species of cormorants breed from September to January. They build their nests from seaweed and any other debris washed up by the sea, usually on the bare ground. Three to five eggs are usually laid. The chicks are born naked but acquire a covering of down within a few days.

# The Osprey

The osprey is not an ocean-going bird with a colony-nesting instinct. Rather it is a solitary bird of prey, patrolling Australia's coastline, flying and gliding in wide circles and figures of eight, eagerly searching the water for fish. Pausing to hover momentarily, it suddenly plummets headlong, wings folded, thrusting its legs forward at the last moment before plunging below the

surface, sending a great shower of water scattering in all directions.

Sometimes it disappears from view, only to reappear, bursting from the surface with tremendous forward strokes of its long wings; at other times it barely skims the surface. Then gaining height, it returns to a favourite perch to eat the fish it has caught.

A number of remarkable adaptations allow the osprey to fish in this way and distinguish it from other birds of prey. Their compact, oily plumage lessens the impact of diving and reduces wetting, their nostrils close under water, a flexible carpal (wrist) joint enables them to sweep the outer wing forward clear of the water. Special adaptations overcome the visual problem of a double image caused by the refraction of light in water. Sharp spicules on the underside of the toes, a reversible outer toe (also present in owls) and highly curved talons help to grasp slippery prey. This last adaptation can occasionally be a disadvantage. Skeletons of ospreys have been found in fisherman's nets, still attached to the fish that apparently drowned them when they were unable to disengage their talons.

Nevertheless, these adaptations have enabled the osprey to become the ecological success that it is, with a world distribution rivalled only by the peregrine falcon. Its anatomical peculiarities are also behind an unresolved controversy over its relationships to other birds of prey. Is it primitive like the kites, with which it shares some characteristics like the absence of the protruding brow that gives many birds of prey their fierce expression, or advanced because of its high degree of specialisation?

With a one metre plus wingspan, dark brown upperparts contrasted with pale underparts and a striking black line separating white throat from pale crown, the osprey is easily identified. It flies on narrow, fingered wings or perches conspicuously on a prominent tree or rock. Invariably associated with water, it nests on inland bodies of freshwater in much of the northern hemisphere.

The Australian subspecies, which also occurs in New Guinea and Southeast Asia, is the only breeding population in the southern hemisphere and is confined to the coastal strip. Only rarely do they venture upstream beyond the influence of the tide. Most

sightings of ospreys away from the coast have been along the large northern rivers and the Murray River, mostly in autumn when young birds are dispersing from breeding areas.

The Australian population, in contrast to some northern hemisphere populations, is non-migratory. Osprey pairs use the same nest year after year, adding sticks and driftwood until it becomes a massive structure about two metres high and two and a half metres wide. These nests are often built in commanding positions, on towering rocky pinnacles, high radio masts, jutting sea cliffs and tall (dead or partly dead) trees. However, particularly where disturbance from man and his animals is negligible, they may simply use boulders or logs just above the high tide mark, or the higher ground of a salt marsh, as the base for their nest.

The osprey's courtship can be quite spectacular. In an undulating flight, the displaying bird makes a series of powerful dives and upward sweeps which may be followed by one of the pair chasing the other. They usually mate at the nest, which they have been busy refurbishing. Both birds bring sticks, sometimes collected in flight by snapping a dead limb off a tree, while the larger female does most of the arranging. Finally they add a lining of seaweed, bark, grass or any other suitable material.

In northern Australia egg laying may begin as early as May, while in southern Australia it begins much later, in September. A clutch of three handsome, boldly marked eggs is laid. After about seven weeks of incubation, during which the female does most of the incubating and the male catches all of the food for the pair, the eggs hatch.

Most Australian ospreys raise two chicks. They hatch in a distinctive patterned, brown down, unlike that of any other bird of prey. This is rapidly covered by the feathers they will keep for their first year, which are similar to those of their parents but browner, more speckled and streaked. Both their plumage and their habit of lying flat in the nest make the chicks quite inconspicuous. They are fed morsels of fish by the female, who also broods them and shelters them from rain and heat by protectively spreading her wings over them. While they are small, the male provides all the food bringing as many as 17 fish a day to the nest.

As they get older, the chicks become more active, vigorously flapping their wings, sometimes rising a short distance from the nest or making short jump-flights into the branches surrounding their nest. During their eighth week they make their first flight away from the nest but return to feed or roost. They may accompany their parents to fishing grounds and are fed the occasional fish by the parents for some weeks after fledging, while they hone their hunting skills. They may not become entirely independent, and move on from their parents territory, for one or two months.

About half of these young ospreys will die in their first year: some become entangled in seaweed and drown; many starve. Their chances of survival are much greater by the time they reach sexual maturity at three years and have possibly found a breeding territory of their own. The oldest known wild osprey was 32.

The osprey's fishing success depends on a number of factors including experience, the abundance of fish in the top one metre of water, and water conditions, particularly clarity. Various studies have shown that they succeed in catching a fish during 25–90 per cent of attempts. They almost exclusively eat live fish, including mullet, tuna, coral trout and garfish. Occasionally they have also been known to capture cuttlefish, sea snakes, frogs, crustaceans and even birds.

Ospreys share Australia's beaches with brahminy kites and white-bellied sea eagles. They each have their own niche.

Elsewhere in the world the osprey sometimes breeds in colonies, with nests only 60–70 metres apart. This habit is probably associated with an abundance of food. In Australia, the closest nests reported were one kilometre apart.

In the early 1800s ospreys could be found right around the Australian coast. Today, they are absent from Tasmania, Victoria and southern New South Wales. Although never common in this corner of Australia, persecution and disturbance had eliminated them by early this century.

Since the 1950s contamination by pesticides may have caused local problems but environmental pollutants have apparently played less of a role in the reduction of osprey numbers in

Australia than they have in the U.S.A. and Europe.

In Australia the osprey is given full protection everywhere, occurs in reasonable numbers over most of its range, and its future seems secure. It is most common on northern Australian beaches, where remoteness probably provides the best protection. In more populated areas, pollutants may cause some breeding failures and deaths, and habitat destruction, especially the removal of large nest trees, is a continuing problem. If left undisturbed, ospreys adapt readily to man and his structures, often nesting on pylons and hunting in front of seaside homes. Greater public awareness can only help the osprey.

## Sea Eagles

There are two other birds of prey that take their food from the ocean. The brahminy kite or red-backed eagle is restricted to the northern half of the continent while the white-bellied sea eagle may be seen soaring over any part of Australia's coastline. It also extends its range into the southern river systems. The kites take a lot of carrion and small creatures stranded by the tide. Sea eagles have a much more varied diet than the osprey, eating, amongst other things, terrestrial mammals, carrion, turtles and birds. They cannot catch fish far below the water's surface and do not dive like the osprey. Notorious pirates, sea eagles may rob an unfortunate osprey of its fish.

## The Frigatebirds

For sheer piracy, the frigatebirds take the cake. Australia has two of the world's six species of frigatebird, the greater, *Fregata minor*, and lesser, *Fregata ariel*, frigatebirds. Both are found in the tropical waters around our north coast but only the lesser frigatebird breeds close to Australia.

The greater frigatebird is a visitor, choosing to breed on distant islands, the closest of which are the Christmas, Cocos-Keeling, and various Coral Sea islands. The lesser frigatebird nests on

islands much closer to the Australian mainland.

In appearance the two birds are quite similar. They have a streamlined body, with lengthy, pointed wings. The tail is long and sharply forked. The beak, like that of most predatory birds, is long and pointed to enable the bird to seize and grasp its prey.

The greater frigatebird is particularly large, reaching a length of up to one metre, while the lesser frigatebird grows to about 65 centimetres. Plumage is similar for both species, but differs between the sexes.

The females have a glossy black body, with white feathers on the chest. In *F. minor*, the throat is blue and naked; in *F. ariel*, it is black. The males are basically black, and are characterised by the distinctive red throat pouch that is inflated during courtship.

When feeding the frigatebird will often harass other birds, such as terns and gulls, to the point that they disgorge their food. The frigatebird then catches the food on the wing, before it lands in the ocean below. As well as this free-loading approach to eating, the frigatebird does employ more conventional methods.

It preys upon fish and squid, which it scoops from the surface of the water, crabs from the shoreline and also the eggs and small chicks of other seabirds.

On the ground it rather resembles a

*ABOVE: A female lesser frigatebird sitting on a nest at Christmas Island. The female frigatebird has a glossy black plumed body with white chest and black throat while the male is black overall, with a red pouch on its throat.*

penguin in its approach to walking. Actually, tiny legs represent only a minor hurdle for frigatebirds, for they spend the greater part of their time in the air. They wheel and dive effortlessly on thermal air currents, always watching the happenings below them, anxious not to miss a free feed.

The frigatebird's flight is possible because the wings have one-third more flying area than any other comparable seabird and are complemented by the skeleton. The wishbone, keel and shoulders fit together perfectly to give support to the flight muscles. The total weight of the frigatebird is unbelievably low, considering its size: an American naturalist calculated that the dried weight was only seven grams!

With a wing span of over two metres, the frigatebird is well suited to spending long periods away from land, but during rough weather it prefers the security of land. Its habit of coming ashore before a storm earned it the name among Aboriginals of 'rain brother'.

In Polynesia, islanders admired the frigatebirds for their amazing powers of flight, and to show their esteem they built tables for the birds at which to feed. Missionaries to the islands used them as an inter-island postal service, by tying messages to their feet. The birds would fly between islands to different feeding tables, where the messages could be removed.

During courtship the male birds are a beautiful sight, as they strut and pout their red throat pouches. Often they will fly low over the nesting grounds with the pouch fully inflated, calling and displaying to any females which care to watch. At the nest the antics continue, as the male and female call to each other with their gaudy, raucous voice.

Preening is a task calling for exceptional flexibility: they land in a tree or on the ground and spread their wings upside down. This allows the sun to dry the under-feathers more efficiently than through the usual methods employed by other birds.

As anyone fortunate enough to have seen the frigatebirds will testify, they cut a truly majestic picture in flight. And, despite their rather unusual table manners, they command our respect as they soar with effortless ease along the northern coast.

# FLAPPERS AND FLIPPERS

*There are a number of birds in Australia that prefer to have their feet on the ground rather than in the air. Most are large birds with strong running legs and a long neck, like the emu and the cassowary, who have given up flight altogether. The endangered bustard, however, will still reluctantly take to the air if absolutely necessary.*

*The penguin is most definitely not a flier. In fact it isn't awfully good on the ground either. It far prefers to swim in the ocean, using its 'wings' as flippers or fins.*

## Emus

The emu takes its name from the Portuguese word 'ema', which means large bird. It is, in fact, the second largest flightless bird in the world, the ostrich taking pride of place. The emus' ancestry is an intriguing puzzle. The emu is the only living member of its family, Dromaiidae, and it belongs to the order of Casuariiformes, along with its relative, the cassowary. Although nobody quite knows whether the emu was ever able to fly, it is generally believed that its predecessors could. Though unproven, it seems likely that the emu has evolved from that early group of flightless birds possibly the same ancestors as the moas. Today the kiwi is the closest surviving member of the moas.

The emu is endemic to Australia and despite constant human interference it remains quite common in isolated areas, especially around farmland.

Unlike the cassowary, the emu prefers a more open landscape. Although some emus display definite migratory patterns, they are chiefly nomadic and follow the food and water supply.

They are often victims of drought as fresh, new grass shoots form a staple part of their diet. In addition they eat flowers, fruits and seeds. In the south west of Western Australia, where zamias are plentiful, the tough outer skins of the cones, are frequently found broken open by the strong emu's beak. The orangy red flesh is relished by emus while for domestic stock it is highly toxic. The fruits of the pestilential prickly pear of Queensland are another favourite. For protein they eat caterpillars, grasshoppers and praying mantis.

Emus are wary birds. They approach water with caution and will only kneel down when entirely at ease. Station workers however have observed that they become accustomed to the same vehicle over a period of time and will only become alarmed when a strange one approaches.

Emus are hopelessly curious and if you dangle or wave a half-hidden object about in front of one, sooner or later it is bound to investigate. They are also quite playful. They have been known to pull the tail of a snoozing farm dog and then run away. They also seem to play tag amongst themselves.

*LEFT: The second tallest flightless bird in the world, the emu is a 'true blue' native of Australia. The father will protect his chicks for two years until they are ready to fend for themselves. Predators of emu chicks include foxes, dingoes and hawks.*

The emu has long and strong legs which will carry it across flat inland plains at over 65 kilometres per hour. When it runs it often flaps its wings — appendages about 20 centimetres long — and uses them as stabilisers. The emu has good eyesight and hearing. To protect the surface of the eye from duststorms it has a special membrane which it pulls across the eye from the inside corner. Another characteristic is its throat pouch. This is not very obvious except in the breeding season. At that time it becomes well-developed and in both the male and female is used to emit a deep booming sound during courtship. A further curious feature of the emu is its three toes, all bearing nails or claws. When an emu is in combat it kicks and the claw is its major form of defence.

Emus display an unusual degree of role reversal. As summer ends the courtship season begins. The dull brown plumage of the female darkens and the pigment of her neck skin becomes a light turquoise-blue. Always the larger of the two, she now dances around the male, fluffing out her wing feathers and making deep-throated booming noises.

Emus' nests vary according to their environment. Some may be no more than trampled down spinifex grass while others are built up 10 centimetres or more above the ground with moss or leaves. Sometimes the site seems dangerously exposed but it is thought that this provides a good vantage-point from which to spot possible predators.

The female lays anything from five to 20 eggs, usually at the rate of one every other day. Each egg weighs up to a kilogram and is about 13 centimetres long. Its shell is about one millimetre thick, though in the north it is said to be thinner. When first laid they are a grainy texture and light green. As incubation continues the eggs darken.

Once all the eggs are laid the male takes over the task of incubation. So dedicated to his task is he that during this time he hardly eats. Once a day, usually at night when the eggs are less prone to predators, he will venture down to the water to drink and on the way he will peck at whatever he can find. During this time he may lose as much as 10 kilograms in weight.

When the chicks are hatched the male continues to be an attentive

father and defends his brood vigorously, although the chicks are well formed when they emerge from the egg and can stand and run about within hours of hatching. Nevertheless they are still easy prey for foxes, dingos, eagles and other hawks. The female often leaves the nest after laying the last egg and usually joins a group of passing emus.

For the next two years the male will protect his chicks until they are full size and ready to breed themselves. Although other females may court the father, he will not enter another breeding cycle until his chicks are off his hands. Until then they wander through the bush in search of food and water. When the pickings are good, emus are very fond of sunbathing and will lie around, apparently quite happily, in stifling heat. They are less able to endure severe cold but they are occasionally spotted at high altitudes.

Emus find a ready food source in the wheatfields. Expanding areas of cleared land and wheat farming have

*ABOVE: Roaming over vast stretches of land in search of food, emus have been known to destroy whole wheat crops either by stripping the ears of wheat and eating them or by trampling the crop. This mainly nomadic species prefers open landscapes, often nesting in apparently highly exposed sites.*

attracted the birds and encouraged population growth. In Western Australia groups of emus have been known to damage entire crops, either by stripping the ears of wheat or simply by trampling it down. As a result the Agriculture Protection Board of Western Australia has erected a 1000 kilometre emu-proof fence designed to protect their farming areas from the emus of the inland. In times of drought hundreds of emus congregate at the fence, blocked in their migration to better grazing. Although emus are surprisingly athletic, able swimmers and capable of climbing fences, this barrier is too high. In 1976 almost 70 000 emus died

Reg Morrison/Weldon Trannies

of starvation at the fence. Since then they have continued to thrive, increasing their population in the good years to compensate for the bad. Further attempts at poisoning and shooting are sanctioned in Western Australia but the problem remains a sticky one.

# Ostriches

As early as the 1860s Australian sheep farmers were realising that neither they nor Australia could ride on the sheep's back forever. So they diversified. As well as raising sheep, they began to raise alpacas, Angora and Kashmir goats — and ostriches. The success of the ostrich venture depended not only on know-how in ostrich-farming but on the fashion in ladies hats. In those days hats trimmed with ostrich feathers were much in favour with modish laides.

The ostrich is the largest of the living birds, a native of the desert and semi-arid zones of Africa and Arabia. The male bird may be 2.5 metres tall and weigh up to 155 kilograms. The neck is long, as are the legs which terminate in two-toed feet, the larger toe with a thick nail. The head is small with a rounded bill and eyes so thickly lashed that mascara seems to have been applied. The bird's coarse body feathers are black in the case of males and brown in females. The beautiful white plumes which make the animal so valuable are part of the tail and small wings. The female is a drab and much smaller creature.

The ostrich is flightless. If threatened, it moves along the ground at speeds of up to 65 kilometres an hour. Normally, the wings are folded when it is in motion. If it cannot outpace its pursuer, it will turn and defend itself with mighty kicks.

The male establishes a harem of about five females for whom he has to fight the other males, a fight accompanied by much roaring and hissing. He then makes the nest, just a shallow indentation in the earth, which he shares with his females.

Each female lays about twelve large white shiny eggs. These are hatched in shifts, the females taking the day and the male the night shift. Incubation takes about 48 days. When the chicks emerge they are about the size of a domestic fowl. At first, the young birds

seem to eat only small stones but after a while they turn to greens. They are vulnerable to attack by other animals. Usually Dad is their protector, but sometimes Dad is savage too, and attacks his own chicks.

People who refuse to recognise unpleasant realities are said to be burying their head in the sand like ostriches. The simile is fallacious. Ostriches don't bury their head in the sand. If danger threatens, the male and his young may lie flat on the sand with neck outstretched to avoid detection. More usually, however, the male would stand and meet any attackers.

It was Samuel, later Sir Samuel, Wilson who imported the first ostriches into Australia. This was in 1869. The birds were sent to his pastoral property in the Wimmera district of Victoria.

The hens laid their eggs in due course; the chicks thrived; and ostrich-farming seemed to have arrived. But then came 'the wet'. Ostriches do not like wet weather, and all the chicks died.

Still, the original birds were doing well. They had been allowed to run wild in a large paddock. When the time came for plucking the feathers there was a débâcle. The birds could not be yarded, since they easily outpaced the fastest horsemen. So an attempt was made to tame the birds. This succeeded but it was too late. By then the beautiful plumes had disappeared.

The dry climate of South Australia was more suitable for ostrich-farming. In 1888 the South Australian Ostrich Company had 510 birds at Port Augusta, where some of their descendants are still around. It was from Port Augusta that birds escaped, where they now run wild, bizarre shapes in an Australian landscape. In New South Wales in the early 1900s there was an ostrich farm near South Head, Sydney, with 100 birds for the plucking. There were other birds at the Hawkesbury Agricultural College, Richmond, where they were being studied. Today, the only ostriches in the State are in zoos.

The Australian ostrich-farming experience was not unique. At the beginning of this century the world-wide value of ostrich-farming was 10 million dollars (U.S.). Today, its value is negligible. Fashion says 'No' to ostrich plumes.

# Cassowaries

When a human encounters a cassowary, the bird is almost always heard before it is seen. The cassowary's response to a strange object, and that includes man, is a low rumbling sound reminiscent of a large truck tearing along a highway. At first approach, the bird stands quite still, watching. If the approach continues and the stranger is getting too close, the cassowary will raise its feathers, stretch to its full height and hiss fiercely. This performance is quite sufficient to hasten the departure of a casual observer. If cornered, the bird will attack but this is seldom the case as cassowaries move easily through thick undergrowth and tangles of vines that would impede man and most other animals.

On occasions when the visitor is too close the bird will walk slowly, but with dignity, away. If chased, however, it crashes through the forest with amazing speed and agility and with little dignity at all.

Cassowaries are closely related to the emu and are found only in Australia and New Guinea. Of the three species, only one — the double-wattled cassowary *Casuarius casuarius* — occurs in Australia, and its range is restricted to tropical rainforest along the east coast of Cape York Peninsula.

When standing erect, the double-wattled cassowary is nearly two metres tall; large individuals weigh about 55 kilograms. The head and throat are covered with bright blue skin that is bare except for a few scattered bristles, and the bare skin at the back of the neck is vivid red, as are the two wattles that dangle some 12 centimetres long from the front of the neck. A laterally flattened bony crown or casque protrudes about 15 centimetres from the top of the head, like a helmet.

The body is covered with long, glossy black plumage which, like that of the emu, has double quills. These feathers, however, are peculiar in that they are little else but quills. These drooping feathers hang at the bird's sides looking like sleek fur, not aviation material.

It is believed, though questionable, that both the plumage and the helmet are adaptations to the dense, thorny undergrowth where cassowaries live. As the bird barges through the bush with head and neck thrust forward, the vegetation is parted by the blade-like helmet or casque and slips easily through the hair-like feathers without catching or tearing them.

The cassowary's dark brown bill is short and strong and the grey-green to horn coloured legs are stout and powerful. The claws are long and strong and that on the innermost of the three toes is elongated to a dagger-like spike. This claw is a deadly weapon in combat when the cassowary leaps feet first at its adversary. Numerous human deaths have resulted from confrontations with cornered cassowaries in New Guinea, and once a European boy was killed by a cassowary in Queensland.

These formidable claws are, however, seldom used. When birds fight each other, they fluff up their feathers, lower their heads down past their bodies, roar loudly and charge each other head-on, leaping into the air and thrusting both feet forward simultaneously. The bout is usually limited to one such attack and little damage is done.

Though some individuals are apparently bad-tempered and unusually aggressive all the time, such aggression is normally displayed only when cassowaries are guarding their nests and chicks. The more common outcome of two males encountering one another is a stretching, rumbling and fluffing contest until one backs down and retires. A female can scare a male away with a much subdued performance — sometimes only quiet staring and a slight stretch — as females are dominant in cassowary society.

Individuals — recognisable by facial characteristics and variations in head and neck coloration and shading — seem to occupy the same areas the year round, and it is believed that they maintain loose feeding territories. During the breeding season, males defend territories of roughly one to three square kilometres, but only close approaches provoke violent aggression.

For most of the year, the female cassowary is solitary, becoming more tolerant of males as the breeding season approaches. She stays with her chosen mate for a few weeks until she is ready to lay, then escorts him to the chosen nest site — a scrape in the ground on the forest floor — where she

*M. F. Soper/A.N.T. Photo Library*

deposits three to eight (usually four) lustrous dark green eggs which fade to pale green during the two month incubation.

Having laid the eggs, the female takes no further interest in the project and abandons her mate to incubate the eggs alone. She may take up to three mates in succession, abandoning each in turn upon egg laying.

Newly hatched cassowaries are, like their emu cousins, longitudinally striped in pale and dark down. The glossy black adult plumage and the ornamental wattles take three years to develop, though the birds may reach sexual maturity before this.

Cassowaries eat mainly fruits that have fallen to the forest floor or have been knocked down by other birds such as fruit pigeons or by arboreal animals such as tree kangaroos. These include figs, quandongs, wild plums and other wild fruits and berries, and the seeds of various palms are also consumed. Some leaves and insects are also ingested and cassowaries will eat fungi, snails, even dead birds, rats and other small carrion. During food shortages in the forests, cassowaries have been known to visit nearby orchards and gardens, eating cultivated fruits such as mulberries, bananas and citrus fruits.

They have regular tracks or runs through the forest, crossing creeks from time to time. They have been seen bathing and appear to be good swimmers. Their routine is leisurely

*ABOVE: This group of ostriches in South Australia can be grateful that fashion nowadays does not value ostrich plumes. First introduced to Australia in 1869 from their native homelands of Africa and Arabia, ostriches were farmed in Victoria and then, South Australia for their plumes. It was in South Australia, that a group escaped to live in the wild.*

and, during observations, they often rested in regular sunny spots from around noon to four in the afternoon.

Cassowaries have few enemies other than man. In New Guinea young cassowaries are eaten and the birds are often raised for food.

The primary threat to cassowaries — as with so many other native animals — is the destruction of their unique and irreplaceable tropical rainforest habitat.

# Fairy Penguins

The spectacle of penguins arriving at dusk on the beach at Phillip Island first received public attention in the late 1920s. It is now estimated that some 250 000 people attend the 'penguin parade' each year and it is undoubtedly one of Victoria's most popular and unusual tourist attractions.

Often thought to be a fish or a mammal, the little or fairy penguin is

Frithfoto/A.N.T. Photo Library

*ABOVE: After tolerating males for the breeding season, leading the father to the nest, and laying three to eight eggs, the female cassowary then abandons her maternal instincts and leaves the male to incubate and rear the chicks. It will take three years for these chicks to develop the glossy black plumage and ornamental wattles similar to those of their parents.*

in fact a bird — but vastly different to other birds. Penguins do not fly and spend much of their lives at sea. Like other birds, they are warm-blooded, have wings and feathers.

In several ways, penguins are more suited to living at sea than on land. The little penguin is well insulated to retain its body heat while staying at sea for long periods but as a consequence may become heat-stressed while ashore in warm weather. Another adaptation of the fairy penguin to its marine environment has been the gradual modification of the wings of its flying ancestors to flippers.

This adaptation has some disadvantages. Penguins cannot fly to avoid predators or search for food. However, they can feed underwater far more effectively than other seabirds. Having legs set well back on the body and the presence of webbed feet increases the swimming efficiency of penguins but makes locomotion on land less efficient; hence the penguin 'waddle'.

The little or fairy penguin is the only one to breed in Australia. It is found in southern coastal waters from Fremantle in Western Australia to southern Queensland. However, the species breeds only along the coast from Carnac Island near Fremantle to near Port Stephens, New South Wales.

Bass Strait is the stronghold of the fairy penguin in Australia although large numbers of other subspecies occur in the North and South Islands of New Zealand and Chatham Islands, east of Christchurch. The birds breed along inaccessible parts of the coastline and offshore islands where mammalian predators cannot kill them.

The main feeding grounds of Phillip Island's little penguins seem to be out in Bass Strait although some birds feed in Western Port and Port Phillip Bays. It is thought that many birds travel between 20 to 50 kilometres each day. However, as they can remain at sea for several days or even weeks at some times of the year, the distances travelled during these periods would be far greater.

Fairy penguins are shallow divers and their recorded swimming speed is 6–8 kilometres per hour. They probably feed in the top 10 metres of the sea although dives of up to 30 metres have been recorded. They feed on fish, mostly pilchards and anchovies but are also partial to Gould's squid.

Those fairy penguins which take part in the Phillip Island 'parade' have a set pattern of behaviour. Just before sunset they move into waters close to the island and form 'rafts' of up to 300 birds. At dusk these 'rafts' move towards the shore and break up into smaller groups which land and cross the beaches. The landing places and paths used through the dunes or up the cliffs seem to be used by the same birds each night.

Once inside the colony, the birds usually preen their feathers or each other and rest for a short period before moving off to their burrows. There is a lot of activity in the colony throughout the night with birds calling and looking for mates, fighting over burrows and searching for burrow sites.

Penguins usually begin breeding in August or September but may start as early as June. Two to three months before breeding, males can be found in the burrows, digging the prospective home, fighting over territory and courting the females.

It appears that females inspect a number of burrows as well as the prospective males before finally choosing a mate. Penguins tend to return to the same part of the colony year after year and occupy burrows usually within a few metres of the one used the previous year, if not the same one. They will also shift to a different burrow after breeding unsuccessfully and are more likely to change mates under these circumstances.

Little penguins usually lay two eggs. These are laid two to four days apart and the first egg is generally dirtier, having been longer in the nest. Incubation of the eggs is shared by both sexes and takes about 35 days. Some penguins lay a second clutch of eggs after raising the first brood or if the first clutch was unsuccessful.

After hatching, the chicks are attended continuously by one or the other parent but about 15 days after hatching the chicks are left unattended and both parents collect food. The chicks go to sea about 7 to 10 weeks after hatching.

The average life expectancy of a breeding penguin is seven years. The oldest breeding bird was a 21-year-old female but it is believed that there is no difference between the survival rates of males and females.

The causes of death of penguins at sea are not well understood but it appears that starvation is more important than predation. However, on land predation by foxes and cats is a significant cause of penguin mortality. The control of these predators is of paramount importance to the survival of little penguins in some areas.

Unlike many seabirds, adult fairy penguins do not migrate large distances and tend to remain relatively close to their breeding colonies even though they may stay at sea for several weeks at a time. There is a pronounced movement to the west of Phillip Island by young penguins in their first year. Most of these young birds feed off the coast between Torquay and Portland before returning to the breeding colony.

During the moulting period when the birds replace their old feathers with new ones, the little penguins remain in the breeding burrows, not necessarily their own. The moult usually takes between 15 and 20 days and during this time the penguins are confined to land as their plumage is not watertight.

# Bustards

The Australian bustard, *Ardeotis australis*, belongs to a group of birds which are distributed through Africa, Asia and Europe. There are 22 species in total, with 18 in Africa, two in Asia, one in Europe and the sole Australian representative. They all prefer to inhabit open, grassy plains. Like the Australian species, most have suffered a decline in numbers, though some African species are still common.

Bustards are typically large, robust birds with a long neck and long, strong legs. The European species has the reputation of being one of the world's heaviest flying bird, weighing up to 16 kilograms. The Australian bustard, also known as the plains or wild turkey, and the African Kori bustard are at least as big as their cousin, if not larger. The males average to about 15–16 kilograms at least while the female is slightly lighter. When standing, the male reaches about 1.2 metres high and the female 0.8 metres.

Bustards have several features which are characteristic of many ground dwelling birds. Their plumage is generally a light brown to cream, which is ideally suited for blending in with the grassy background. Whereas birds that perch in trees have four toes, the bustard has only three forward facing toes. The hind toe is absent as it would serve no purpose for a bird living on the ground.

Because of their heavy weight, bustards require a considerable distance in which to become airborne. This may be one reason why they prefer the open country, free of trees which could restrict their take-off. Once in the air, they move their two metre wingspan

*LEFT: Hand-feeding cassowaries is all very well but it can be hazardous for both birds and humans. This practice, attractive to tourists, lures the birds out of their habitat and into contact with dangers such as dogs and cars. From the human point of view, cassowaries have been known to kill people who stray too close to their nest.*

Peter Dann/A.N.T. Photo Library

R. & D. Keller/A.N.T. Photo Library

*ABOVE: Coming ashore at night during summer to waddle to the sand dunes and make their burrows, fairy penguins are the smallest penguins in the world.*
*LEFT: This rocky shoreline offers a further obstacle to the fairy penguins whose flippers and webbed feet which are set well back on the body make movement on land awkward.*

with a slow, heavy movement and rarely fly above 100 metres. This contrasts with many large birds such as the pelican and eagle who rise to thousands of metres on the air thermals.

Generally, bustards are reluctant flyers, taking to the air only as a last resort should danger be present. They prefer a more casual retreat from danger. First they 'freeze' and then walk away with their neck stretched out and their head erect. Sometimes they will take advantage of their dull plumage and squat on the ground. Young birds incapable of flight are particularly adept at using this method.

Prior to mating, the male performs a spectacular courtship display. He inflates the loose skin at the front of his neck to form an 'apron' which almost touches the ground. At the same time he lifts his tail forward so that it touches the back of his head. The performance is completed by the bird drooping its wings and strutting along uttering deep booming calls.

The breeding season is highly variable but is strongly tied to the period of greatest grass growth. In northern Australia it is mainly in the late wet and early dry season, January to March. In southern Australia September to November is the usual time. Rather than forming a bonded pair it is believed the male wanders off and leaves the female to incubate the eggs and protect the young chicks. She lays one, though sometimes two, on bare ground. Little attempt is made to construct a nest but occasionally a few pieces of grass are laid down. Sometimes the eggs are placed near a bush which would provide a minimal amount of protection. As with other ground dwelling birds, the eggs are a cryptic coloration of olive brown and green with similar coloured spots.

Despite the excellent camouflage, the eggs are still found and eaten by predators. Foxes and dingoes are the main offenders. One bird-of-prey, the black-breasted kite, also has a liking for the eggs. After frightening the female off the nest, the kite picks up a stone or piece of earth, and drops the 'bomb' on the eggs. The kite then feeds on the shattered remains and sometimes carries the broken shells to its nest.

An increase in numbers of the bustard seems to be a slow process. Males do not begin breeding until about five or six years of age and the female at about two or three years. Combine this with the small number of eggs laid and it is no wonder that the bustard has been unable to cope with changes in habitat and shooting pressures over the last 200 years.

The Aborigines prized the bustard as an excellent source of meat. Because of its unwillingness to fly, the Aborigines could easily stalk the bird and spear it. Another method involved the men forming a large circle around a flock and lighting a fire. Once the smoke confused the birds the men were able to knock them down using boomerangs or nulla nullas.

Although bustards eat insects, small reptiles and mammals, their preference is for seeds, leaves and fruits of various plants. In northern Western Australia the bustard has a particular liking for the fruits of the moonflower bush, *Capparis spinosa*. The Aborigines were aware of this and were known to catch the bustards in pits dug around these plants.

The population of the bustards was probably never threatened by the actions of the Aborigines. But the arrival of the Europeans in 1788 bought about changes that did affect the population. At the time of settlement, bustards were found in open country throughout the mainland of Australia. As with many Australian animals, the bustard could not compete with the hordes of sheep and cattle and their voracious appetites. Bustards suffered even more when rabbits were released in 1859 and further pressure was placed on them by people who hunted them for their meat.

Today the bustard is most common in north-east Queensland and there are indications that their numbers may be increasing in that region. Western Australia also supports reasonable numbers though they are mainly found in the more remote parts well away from human disturbance.

Excellent research is being done in Victoria with the aim of reintroducing the bustard back into national parks and select farming areas in that State. We can only hope that such research is successful and that these magnificent birds will be seen again in areas they once roamed. To quote from a New South Wales National Parks and Wildlife Service poster about the bustard, let's 'give the poor bustard a go!'

Bay Picture Library

---

*RIGHT: 'Give the poor bustard a go!' was the NSW National Parks and Wildlife Services' campaign to save the bustard whose numbers had severely declined. This was due to their habitat of open grasslands being invaded by cattle, sheep, humans, rabbits and predators such as foxes and humans.*
*BELOW: Flight for the bustard is a reluctant procedure, usually only undertaken as a last resort to fleeing from danger.*

G. Deichmann/Auscape Int.

# THE KINGFISHER CLAN

*Kingfishers are birds of great beauty but unusual form. Their plumage is kinglike, a mixture of regal colours. Such beauty is not matched by their form: the long beak is wildly disproportionate to the small fat body, short legs and stumpy tail.*

*There is one kingfisher family in Australia, the Alcedinidae, with two subfamilies, the Daceloninae and the Alcedininae. Birds of the two groups follow different mating and nesting patterns.*

## The True Kingfishers

Kingfishers belong to the Alcedinidae family of which there are two subfamilies, Daceloninae and Alcedininae. In the latter subfamily, there are only two Australian members: the azure kingfisher, *Ceyx azureus*, and the little kingfisher, *C. pusillus*, both of which fish for their food.

These two species take up a position on a river bank or on the branch of a tree stretching over a river and watch the water intently, occasionally bobbing the head, perhaps in impatience.

When a victim approaches they 'freeze'. Then they dive down, seize it in the beak and, with a powerful upward push of their wings, propel themselves from the water. They carry the fish back to their perch and eat it head first.

The azure kingfishers have beautiful violet plumage on the upper body. They are common around inland

*Bay Picture Library*

*RIGHT: A sacred kingfisher with prey. BELOW: Three beautifully plumed young azure kingfishers. Azure kingfishers are common around waterways inland from the north western Western Australia coast through to Victoria.*

*Glen Threlfo/ Auscape Int.*

G. Chapman/Auscape Int.

*ABOVE: The little kingfisher is a shy, solitary bird which lives around water in the mangrove and rainforest areas of northern Queensland and the Northern Territory.*
*LEFT: A red-bellied black snake meets its demise as this laughing kookaburra prepares to swallow it whole.*

waterways all along the coast from the north-west of Western Australia to Victoria, and are also found in Tasmania. The little kingfishers have a remote north-western distribution, and are hardly ever seen, a fact explained not only by their range but by their nature. They are shy, solitary birds which fly low over water.

When the birds pair, they nest in a chamber at the end of a tunnel excavated in the sandy bank of a stream. The birds excavate by flying at the bank at high speed with beak outstretched, and sometimes a beak is

broken in the process. The displaced earth is pushed out of the tunnel, the birds using their feet for the job.

Before mating the couple practices a feeding rite. As the female sits upright in the nest, beak in the air and chirping plaintively, the male presents her with a fish which she eats. The two incubate the eggs on a bed composed of, or surrounded by, disgorged fish bones and, not unnaturally, the atmosphere in the nuptial chamber is malodorous.

# Forest-dwelling Kingfishers

Birds of the subfamily, Daceloninae are forest-dwellers, birds whose habitat may be far from water. Their food is mostly small reptiles or insects although they will occasionally eat fish also. Some birds of the genus *Halcyon* do feed on sandbanks near freshwater streams, where, on a good day, fish may fall victim to their dives.

They are smaller than the Daceloninae, ranging in size from 18 to 25 centimetres, and their tails and bills are shorter. Only their colouring is typical: it is the unmistakable royal blue and turquoise of the kingfishers. Their cry is not a laugh but a harsh shriek.

Australian species include the forest kingfisher, *Halcyon macleayii*, named for W. S. Macleay, the 19th century British naturalist; the sacred kingfisher, *H. sancta*, which occurs in New Zealand as well as in Australia, the mangrove kingfisher, *H. chloris*, and the red-backed kingfisher, *H. pyrrhopygia*.

## The kookaburra

Kookaburras range through woodlands along the east, southeast and southwest coast of Australia, are the best known members of the Daceloninae group. There are two species, the laughing kookaburra, *Dacelo novaehollandiae*, and the more colourful blue-winged kookaburra, *D. leachii*. Both are rather stocky birds up to 46 centimetres in length, with a large head and a strong heavy bill 6.5 to 7.7 centimetres long. Their breeding, nesting and feeding habits are

*ABOVE: The colourful blue-winged kookaburra features sky-blue cloured wings and rump, a darker blue tail, a cream head streaked with brown, a brown back and cream belly. Colouration, habitat and voice are the differences between the blue-winged and laughing kookaburras.*
*RIGHT: A forest kingfisher, featuring the distinctive royal blue and turquoise colouring. Forest-dwelling kingfishers have longer tails than their relatives of the waterways.*

seen to snatch goldfish from garden ponds. Even a picnic in the bush is likely to attract a group of kookaburras who will wait patiently for a tidbit to be thrown their way.

Active by day, kookaburras feed on insects, small mammals, lizards, snakes, small birds and eggs, generally swooping down abruptly on their hapless prey, snatching it in their powerful beaks and beating it to death against the ground or a branch. Birds have been seen mistakenly battering pieces of rope, string or spaghetti.

The somewhat maniacal-sounding song of the kookaburra is one of the most familiar and well-loved sounds of the Australian bush, earning it the name 'bushman's clock'. To the ears of the early European settlers however, its call sounded strange and sinister; the explorer Charles Sturt called it 'a chorus of wild spirits'. The raucous, laughing song is actually the kookaburra's territorial proclamation, heard mostly at dawn and dusk but also throughout the day when birds inadvertently stray into each other's territories. When one bird starts to sing, others in the neighbourhood join in, creating at times a deafening cacophony. A fairly wide repertoire of chuckling calls can be heard and a staccato squawk signals alarm. The blue-winged kookaburra's song is higher and more rapid than the laughing kookaburra's, sometimes described as a 'howl' rather than a 'laugh'.

In good conditions kookaburras may live for twenty years or more and they mate for life. Unlike most kingfishers, they are sedentary, occupying the same territory all year round. They breed mostly between September and January, the female laying two or three eggs after a brief courtship. No nests are built, the eggs being laid in any hollow large enough to accommodate an adult bird. Termite mounds, particularly favoured by the blue-winged kookaburra, and tree hollows are the most usual nesting sites but holes in river banks or even niches in buildings may be used.

similar but they differ in colouration and habitat.

The laughing kookaburra has a white head with a dark streak through the eye and onto the temple, and a white throat, breast and belly. The back is dark brown, the wings are brown with a sky-blue patch, and the white-tipped tail is banded with black and brown. The blue-winged kookaburra has a cream head streaked with brown, a brown back and cream belly. The rump and wings are sky-blue and the tail a darker blue.

Originally the laughing kookaburra occurred only in mainland eastern Australia from central Cape York Peninsula to Eyre Peninsula in South Australia. About the turn of the century,

however, it was introduced into Tasmania and southwestern Western Australia, and also to New Zealand, where quite large populations quickly acclimatised. The blue-winged variety lives in the northern and northeastern coastal fringes of Australia and in New Guinea. It prefers wetter areas, such as paperbark swamps, than its more common relative but their ranges overlap in many parts of Queensland.

The preferred habitat of these birds is open woodland and forest, but they are highly adaptable and have moved into farmland, orchards and even city parks and gardens. Those living in populated areas often become quite tame. Many a suburban garden has its regular visitors and birds have been

After a twenty-four day incubation period the hatchlings emerge and fledge after thirty-six days. The fledglings are fed for a further eight to thirteen weeks and unlike most other birds do not leave to establish their own territories but stay with the family in non-breeding, auxiliary roles for up to four years. They help to feed and protect subsequent broods and to defend the family's territory. Such a long nurturing period means that more than one brood per season is unlikely.

Although in many ways this distinctive social system enhances the kookaburras' survival chances, their low reproductive rate makes them very vulnerable to such potential dangers as habitat destruction and misuse of pesticides. They have already been threatened by DDT which, building up in their food chain, causes their eggs to be thin-shelled and easily broken.

G. Chapman/Auscape Int.

# Other Kingfishers

Apart from the three genera already mentioned, there are two species sufficiently different to warrant separate classification. Both are closely related to the Halcyon species. The yellow-billed kingfisher, *Syma torotoro*, is probably the least known of Australian kingfishers. An inhabitant of tropical rainforests in Cape York, it may be partly migratory, travelling between Australia and islands further north. In most respects it seems to resemble the sacred kingfisher.

The most beautiful of Australian kingfishers is undoubtedly the white-tailed kingfisher, *Tanysiptera sylvia*.

This gorgeously coloured species, with a long white tail, arrives in northern Queensland from New Guinea in November for the breeding season. By the end of April they have all returned. At the start of the season the birds are constantly on the move, jostling for territories and nesting sites. The pace tapers off towards the end of the season, allowing them to gain some condition for the flight back to New Guinea.

# SEASONAL VISITORS

*The migration of many species of birds is one of the greatest phenomenons of the natural world. Through sheer instinct, many migratory birds are able to maintain flight paths, often over enormous tracts of sea or desert, even at night, without landmarks to guide them. Many ornithologists now believe that some migratory birds navigate astronomically using the sun, the moon and/or the stars as a guide.*

Until 1953, when the Australian Bird Banding Scheme was set up, very little was known about bird migration in Australia. The exact number of species that undertake migration to and from Australia is still not known, but a large number of species are involved in migration to varying degrees.

Migratory birds are extremely mobile, and are able to utilise the benefits of two different environments, during the seasons that suit them best. One of these environments is usually occupied for breeding, and the other used to support them for the rest of the year. Food supply is often one of the major reasons for bird migration, coupled with climatic conditions.

The influences that lead to restlessness and 'flocking', signs of readiness for migration, are caused not only by external factors such as climate, but also, and more importantly, through internal changes. These changes often relate to changes in the birds' reproductive physiology.

Even within single species of birds these migrational cues vary. This sometimes leads to 'partial migration', where even in the same area, younger birds tend to be more migratory than older ones.

Within Australia, migration is not as marked as in continents such as Europe, where the seasons are much more extreme.

A number of birds cross the Equator annually, from Australia to northern Asia, to breed. These journeys are thought to have stemmed from ancient times, when Australia and Asia were closely linked by land masses.

T. & P. Gardner/A.N.T. Photo Library

## Plovers and Dotterels

The grey plover, *Pluvialis squatarola*, and the eastern golden plover, *P. dominica*, are both seasonal visitors to Australia. They spend spring and summer in Australia, before flying north for the northern summer. There they breed on the Siberian and Arctic tundras. Unlike the other plovers, these two birds are confined almost solely to the seashore. They will sometimes fly several kilometres inland to rest between feeding sessions, but all their feeding takes place along the

*ABOVE: Its name belies its place of origin; the Mongolian dotterel is a native of Siberia and not of Mongolia. This bird breeds in Siberia and flies to Australia searching for food in sandy coastal areas usually in the northern region of Australia.*

waterline. There they forage for small invertebrates along sand and mud flats and in rocky areas. The grey plover, also called the black-bellied plover, is well known for its wistful song.

Belonging to the same family as the plovers are the dotterels. Not all dotterels are such enthusiastic wanderers. There are five species which are resident in Australia all year round, but four of the species are migratory.

Probably the most familiar is the double-banded dotterel, *Charadrius bicinctus*. These small birds, about 18 centimetres in length, arrive in Australia in March and April from their breeding grounds in New Zealand. They quickly spread themselves all around the southern and eastern coastline. They can be found as far north as the Tropic of Capricorn in the east, and Perth in the west. They generally avoid the central areas of the Great Australian Bight.

Large flat areas are favoured by this bird, and where there are sizeable inland lakes they will congregate on the shores, quickly darting along in an effort to capture a meal of insects or invertebrates.

A less familiar bird is the large-billed dotterel, *C. leschenaultii*. This bird spends summer in Australia before migrating to central and eastern Asia to breed in the northern summer. Birds which are late in leaving for the breeding grounds will often attain full breeding plumage before they depart. Black markings appear on the crown and ears and a bright orange breast band develops.

The Oriental dotterel, *C. veredus*, is another visitor from Asia. A small, active bird, it is seen along Australian shores and in inland northern Australia during our summer and spring, leaving for China and Mongolia in early autumn. Very little is known of its habits, not because of any scarcity, but because there are few research facilities in its range.

Despite its name, the Mongolian dotterel, *C. mongolus*, is not a native of Mongolia. It breeds on Siberian tundras and migrates to Australia for the southern summer. It can often be seen in the company of the double-banded dotterel, and is sometimes confused with this bird. In non-breeding plumage the two birds are quite similar.

B. Chudleigh/A.N.T. Photo Library

T. & P. Gardner/A.N.T. Photo Library

# Other Migratory Waders

The bar-tailed godwit, *Limosa lapponica*, and the black-tailed godwit, *L. limosa*, which both breed in Siberia, are best known for their long, probing bills which they sink in mud in search of aquatic worms and molluscs. Both inhabit coastal areas, around mudflats and estuaries.

There is some question as to how the great knot, *Calidris tenuirostris*, another visitor from Siberia came by its unusual name. It is said to be a corruption of the word Canute, based on the legend of King Canute. This is because of the bird's habit of running to follow the ebb of the tide.

The range of the great knot extends from Japan to Siberia. Like the black-tailed godwit, the great knot is fairly rare in Australia. From August to March the bird inhabits most coastal areas of Australia. There is very little scientific knowledge about the movements of the bird.

The main breeding grounds of the northern, or red-necked phalarope, *Phalaropus lobatus*, range from Siberia to Alaska. These small aquatic waders usually migrate to areas such as northern New Guinea. The birds only reach Australia when they veer from their usual paths, often due to disturbances such as cyclones.

Like many other migratory birds,

the marsh sandpiper, *Tringa stagnatilis*, spends its winters in such warm climates as Africa, Indonesia and India, as well as Australia. Ornithologists are still not certain where the birds breed, but it is believed to be in an area which stretches from Central Europe to Mongolia. From August to March, the marsh sandpiper inhabits various inland water regions of Australia.

Another wader, the terek sandpiper, *T. terek*, is distinguished by its upturned bill and bright orange legs. The bird is fairly common in northern Australia. It breeds in an area which extends from the Arctic, through Finland to Siberia. The terek sandpiper is well known for its breeding courting song, which during the peak of the courting period can be heard over several days. In Australia the bird inhabits coastal water areas, around mudflats and mangroves.

Other visitors from Siberia include

*TOP LEFT: The ruddy turnstone, so named because it turns over stones when searching for food.*
*ABOVE: The eastern curlew keeps a low profile, migrating to Australia from Siberia at night.*

the whimbrel, *Numenius phaeopus*, and the little whimbrel, *N. minutus*. The little whimbrel is distinguished by its fearless nature. Because it does not fly away until directly threatened, it is easy prey for hunters. Like other migratory waders, the whimbrels feed around mudflats in search of aquatic worms and molluscs.

Scientific records concerning the migratory path of the eastern curlew, like the records concerning so many other migratory birds are far from complete. It is believed that the eastern curlew, *Numenius madagascariensis*, migrates by night, as there have been

Graeme Chapman/Auscape Int.

*LEFT: The pallid cuckoo is partly migratory, moving up and down Australia each year.*
*BOTTOM: The golden bronze cuckoo mainly uses the nests of warblers and fantails. This cuckoo, quite common in Australia, breeds in the south of the continent.*

very few sightings of the bird making its journey to Australia for the northern winter. Interestingly on the return flight to Siberian breeding grounds, the birds fly very conspicuously by day.

The eastern curlew is distinguished by its long bill which is used for probing mudflats and beaches for food. Although the eastern curlew resembles the whimbrel and little whimbrel, with its mottled dark brown and white body colouring and similar shape, its bill is much longer.

The grey-tailed tattler, *Tringa brevipes*, breeds in northern Asia and winters around northern Australia. It is one of the most common migratory waders, occasionally found as far south as Tasmania. The grey-tailed tattler tends to nest in extremely mountainous regions, so little is known of its nesting habits.

Australia also has a number of Japanese visitors, including the Japanese snipe, *Gallinago hardwickii* and the flesh-footed shearwater, *Puffinus carneipes*. The flesh-footed shearwater actually breeds in Australia, in areas such as Lord Howe Island and occasionally on islands in the Indian Ocean. The birds spend their summers around Japan. These dark water birds are considered a pest to line fishermen, as they dive among the lines for fish.

The Japanese snipe is another long-billed wader. Like the Chinese snipe, the Japanese snipe is prized by hunters because of its fast erratic flight, which challenges marksmen to test their skill. Although the population of the bird has decreased in Australia due to destruction of swampland and other natural habitats of the bird, the population has increased around Taiwan and Japan. Fortunately large flocks of Japanese snipe still reach Australia's eastern coast, Victoria and Tasmania.

The knot, *Calidris canutus*, the Arctic skua, *Stercorarius parasiticus* and the ruddy turnstone, *Arenaria interpres* all breed in the Arctic regions and winter in Australia. The ruddy turnstone is so

Graeme Chapman/Auscape Int.

called because of its feeding methods: this lively bird turns over stones and shells with its bill in search of food.

# The Cuckoos

As well as the great variety of birds which regularly cross the equator, often travelling extremely long distances, there are a number of birds that travel to Australia from neighbouring areas such as New Zealand and New Guinea.

A regular traveller between New Zealand and the Solomon Islands, the shining bronze cuckoo, *Chrysococcyx lucidus lucidus*, often veers off course to areas along Australia's east coast, such as Lord Howe Island. Like many of its relatives, this small, swift bird has a clear call, often heard at night.

The channel-billed cuckoo, *Scythrops novaehollandiae*, also known as stormbird or rainbird, usually arrives in northern Australia before the annual rains. This long-tailed, raucous bird winters in areas around New Guinea. It is the largest of the parasitic Australian cuckoos, measuring about 60 centimetres in length, of which 8 centimetres is taken up by the huge bill.

Channel-billed cuckoos are found in Australia from spring to autumn, and occur over most of the monsoon area. They move a considerable distance south, usually as far as Sydney, and have even been recorded in Tasmania.

Large stands of tall trees are required by the channel-billed cuckoo, and it can often be seen flying lazily over the tree-tops emitting its loud raucous cry. This habit earned the name hornbill from early settlers, who mistook it for a relative of the hornbill found from Africa through to New Guinea.

Channel-billed cuckoos breed in Australia, and generally choose the nest of a crow in which to lay their eggs. Other hosts include currawongs, magpies and the collared sparrowhawk. Young channel-bills do not seem to eject other nestlings from the nest. This is possibly because more than one channel-billed cuckoo may occur in each nest, and random ejection would not help the species whatsoever. However, the female often makes up for this by ejecting one of the hosts eggs when she lays her own.

Many cuckoos, such as the pallid cuckoo, are at least partly migratory, moving up and down the continent each year. The pallid cuckoo is found over all of Australia, contracting its range during the winter months. The oriental cuckoo, *Cuculus saturatus*, is a non-breeding visitor to Australia, arriving in northern Australia in November and departing in April.

In most respects the oriental cuckoo is bigger than the pallid cuckoo, and it might be thought that competition between the two species could develop. But shortly before the oriental cuckoo arrives in the north, the pallid cuckoo moves south to breed; in late summer the process is reversed, with the pallid cuckoo returning north again, and the oriental cuckoo migrating back to its breeding sites in Melanesia and southeast Asia.

The rufous-tailed bronze cuckoo, *Chrysococcyx basalis*, also known as Horsfield's cuckoo, is a partly migratory species found all over Australia in lightly timbered country.

# Swallows

In the northern hemisphere swallows are hailed with delight as the harbingers of spring, the 'glad prophets of the year'. In Australia their arrival is greeted less rapturously. With our equable climate, the coming of spring passes almost unnoticed and, in any case, different species of swallow appear in different areas at different seasons. Indeed, some Australians find swallows obnoxious because of their slovenly nesting behaviour, though they admit to enjoying the birds' gay song.

All members of this family are small, the largest no longer than 17 centimetres. Their wings, while tiny, are sturdy and the birds are spectacular flyers. On the ground they move awkwardly — but then the ground is not their medium.

Swallows are noted for their long migrations. The great eighteenth-century naturalist, Gilbert White, did not believe that such seemingly frail birds were capable of intercontinental migrations. He was mistaken. A species such as the barn swallow, which breeds in North America and Europe, may spend the winter in the tropics in, say, South America, Africa or Asia.

Most native birds were adversely affected by white settlement which cleared their woodland habitat for agriculture. Not so the welcome

*BELOW: Unlike most native birds, the welcome swallow has actually increased in numbers since white settlement in Australia. These birds use man-made constructions such as bridges, buildings, and dam walls for their nesting places.*

B. Chudleigh/A.N.T. Photo Library

swallows, *Hirundo neoxena*, whose numbers have actually increased since settlement.

They thrive in open country, and human dwellings have provided them with nesting places. Their nest is often a cup, fashioned from mud and vegetation, which they plaster onto the walls of buildings. Often a pair returns each year to the same nest to produce more than one brood. Both male and female cooperate in incubating the eggs and in raising the young, which emerge from the eggs after about fifteen days and fledge in a further twenty.

The barn swallows, *Hirundo rustica*, are not endemic, but visit northern Australia during the monsoons. Before they migrate they seem to throw a farewell party: hundreds of them gather as darkness is falling and roost near the water.

Swallows and martins feed on insects captured in flight. Their mouth, with its very wide gape forms an effective insect trap.

They are of importance to man because the insects on which they feed are those marked for eradication by

*ABOVE: The barn swallow migrates over long distances; it breeds in North America and Europe and travels to South America, Asia, Africa and occasionally Australia to spend the northern winter.*

---

man: flies, mosquitoes and gnats as well as many others which attack crops.

# Rainbow Bee-eaters

For southern Australians the rainbow bee-eater shares the same habit as the northern hemisphere swallow, arriving around the beginning of spring. Its winter habitat includes New Guinea, the Sunda and Solomon Islands with some flocks remaining in northern Australia. There, the immature birds grow adult plumage over the winter, but none of these breed. This is reserved for the south.

There, like the swallows, the rainbow bee-eater prefers lightly wooded areas or open spaces where telephone

lines provide resting places between feeding flights. The bird's flight is erratic but graceful, adapted to sudden lunges as it finds its prey. Its staple diet is any insect but with a preference for dragonflies as well as bees and hornets.

With a plumage dominated by green and highlighted with blue, buff, yellow and black, the 20 centimetre long rainbow bee-eater has earned its impressive title in two languages, *Merops ornatus*. Merops is Greek for bee-eater and ornatus, Latin for adorned. However other names, such as berrin-berrin, gold-digger and plain bee-eater testify to the popularity of this small bird.

One peculiarity of the species is its immunity to both bee and wasp stings. Over a day a single bird may eat several hundred bees or other insects and because of its vigorous flying patterns the body requires this level of input. The moisture supplied by its prey is also sufficient for its fluid needs and the birds seldom, if ever, require water.

However, streams play their part during the mating season. The male

NPIAW

*LEFT: The black-faced monarch is a true sun follower; spending summer in southeastern Australia, autumn in northern Queensland and winter in New Guinea. Both parents partake in building the nest and feeding the young when they hatch.*

The six Australian species certainly follow the flycatcher prototype in their physical make-up. They are small, only 12 to 20 centimetres long, with a tail which appears elongated in relation to the tiny body. Their short wide flattened bill is slightly curved at the end, and their mouth is surrounded with bristles through which insects are funnelled into the wide gape. Their colouring is drab. The body is grey, or black and white — with not a touch of the imperial purple or crimson which might be expected in a bird with the title 'monarch'. Only the head is eye-catching. Dark marks on the pale face create the illusion that the bird is wearing a mask.

## Body language

During the courtship period the males fly through the forest, singing lustily. Both male and female co-operate in building the nest. This is usually cup-shaped, its material varying with species.

The females lay two to four eggs in a clutch, the eggs generally white or brown. The incubation period varies from 14 to 15 days. As one bird broods the eggs, its partner feeds it. During this period the black-faced monarch warns off intruders by advertising its territory with the loud call 'Why you, Why you'. When the eggs hatch one parent passes part of its food to its importunate offspring.

The young birds do not have the dark face marks of the adults. These seem to appear as part of the growing-up process, with their colour intensifying as sexual maturity approaches.

The black-faced monarch inhabits the length of the eastern coastal strip of Australia, from Cape York to the most southerly tip of Victoria, though it does not appear in Tasmania. The spectacled monarch occupies the same strip but only as far south as just beyond the New South Wales border. The black-winged monarch only occupies the rainforests of the most northerly stretch of this strip on Cape York Peninsula.

and female, whose plumage renders them almost indistinguishable to the human eye, prefer their sandy banks where they tunnel their nests, sometimes as long as one metre. The eggs, when laid, rest in a larger chamber at the end of the burrow and number around five, but may vary between three and seven. Their colour is white with a sheen which renders the shell almost translucent. Predators would find difficulty attacking the nesting hen since the tunnel is no wider than the narrow circumference of the bird's body.

During the period of mating and nesting, the normally gregarious rainbow bee-eater prefers the company of its mate and this pattern may continue until the nestlings are ready to fly.

The general migration north of these birds begins around March and April. Then the characteristic high pitched chatter as the flocks gather is a sign of the coming winter.

# Monarch Flycatchers

Some species of monarch flycatchers move around so much that ornithologists have difficulty in charting their migrations. Like human jet-setters, the monarchs follow the sun. Some of them, including the black-faced monarch and the spectacled monarch, spend the summer months in southern Australia. In autumn they move north to Queensland and, in the winter, to New Guinea. The black-winged monarch is restricted to Cape York.

Monarchs occur in the southern hemisphere mainly in Africa, New Guinea, South Pacific and Australia. Some are also found in India, Southeast Asia and Japan. In the Australian area at least six species have been identified, most of them confined to northern Queensland. They are members of the flycatcher family.

Flycatchers are small lively birds with a bill curved at the end and a long tail. They feed on insects which they take on the wing. After each sortie they return to the branch to await the arrival of another flying titbit. This description applies to most of the monarchs.

Some however, depart from the family pattern. The black-faced monarch, *Monarcha melanopsis* and the spectacled monarch, *M. trivirgatus* do not take insects on the wing like their relatives, but seek them on the branches, trunks and leaves of trees in the middle layers of the forest.

# SOUNDS OF THE BUSH

*Most birds sing, or at least make noises of some kind, but in the Australian bush there are some musical sounds which quite surpass the average songster. Some of these birds, like the whipbird and bellbird, are more easily heard than seen. Others, like the tuneful magpies and rollicking currawongs, are everyday sights. No matter how common or obscure, the members of the Australian bird orchestra are a constant source of delight.*

# Magpies

One of the most melodic sounds in the Australian bush may be heard at dawn and dusk as the magpie chorus assembles to advertise and defend its territory. And, in between recitals, these great entertainers will keep the watcher amused with their intriguing antics.

Magpies, *Gymnorhina tibicen*, are Australian natives which were introduced to New Zealand. Their sturdy body, about 45 centimetres long, is supported on long black legs. The beak, a bluish grey, is tipped with black and only very slightly hooked at the end. Plumage varies according to race, but is basically black relieved by white patches.

There are six races of magpie divided into three major subdivisions. Five of these races can be found in Australia, formerly classified as distinct species. But the fact that they are able to interbreed precludes their being classified as separate species. The black-backed magpie, *G. tibicen tibicen*, which occurs over most of Australia north of the Murray River, central South Australia and Shark Bay, Western Australia, has white markings on the nape, rump, tail and wing shoulders. The white-backed magpie, *G. tibicen hypoleuca*, is similar, but has white on the back; it is found throughout southeastern Australia, including Tasmania. The western magpie, *G. tibicen dorsalis*, is confined to the southwest corner of the continent; in most respects this race is similar to the white-backed magpie.

Early settlers called these birds magpies after the familiar birds of their homeland. However the Australian magpie has nothing in common with the European magpie other than colouration. The quality of the magpie's call far surpasses that of the European crows and magpies, and earned for it the alternative names of flute bird, organ bird and piper.

*PREVIOUS PAGE: The Australian magpie is one of the best known of this country's birds. This is the black-backed form.*
*TOP: The female Australian magpie (white-backed form) varies from the male in that it has a grey back.*
*RIGHT: A male Australian magpie (white-backed form) guards over its nest.*

108

T. & P. Gardner/A.N.T. Photo Library

*ABOVE: The pied currawong with its yellow eyes, white patches on its rump and the tip of its tail, produces the noises 'curra-wa', 'chilla-wong' and 'curra-wong' from which this species' name is derived.*
*LEFT: Growing to about 50 centimetres long, the grey currawong is slightly larger than the pied currawong.*

Magpies, like the bowerbirds, seem fascinated by shining objects. They will sometimes decorate their nests with articles such as spoons and even diamond rings. The reason for their 'interior design' tastes is not known, but it is not advisable to leave valuables lying around at the start of the breeding season — usually around August.

Some magpies, such as the western magpie, are groupies. As many as 24 birds live together and cooperate in defending their territory against other birds, particularly members of their own species. With other races, groups are much smaller.

The group feeds together, mostly on the ground, the birds using their stout bill to unearth grubs and beetles. When they travel they move in one noisy flock.

Females become physically capable of breeding when they are one year old, but they may not get the opportunity to do so until they are about five. The older females breed first, a pattern distinctly different from that observed in human society.

Bay Picture Library

109

Breeding time is from August to October. Only one male is privileged to father the brood. Other mature males with the mating urge will try to attract the attention of the females and, if the latter are coy, their would-be seducers may get rough.

Despite this rampant sexuality, there is usually only one successful nest in the group, an untidy container formed of sticks and lined with grass or other soft substance, placed high in trees such as eucalypts. Alternatively, the nest may be made from pieces of wire and placed on telegraph poles. This is a procedure guaranteed to damage the lines. However, the Electricity Department appears to take a very paternalistic view of such goings on, merely removing the nests to more suitable locations.

The female also incubates the eggs alone, which takes about twenty days. There may be as many as six eggs which are blue or green, and blotched and streaked with brown.

The reason why there is only one successful nest is that the dominant male is usually incapable of feeding more than one female, and even the favoured female isn't overfed. As well as feeding 'his' bird, the male has a lot of other duties on his agenda: he must keep the other members of the group in order, and he must look to the defence of their territory.

The young stay in the nest until they are about four weeks old. Even then, they cannot fly properly and must beg food from their elders for about two months. Their hunger is indicated by piteous wails. For the first twelve months of their lives, and sometimes into the second year, the young are dusky replicas of the adults. Their black markings are a little dull, and their white feathers a smokey grey.

Magpies are notorious for their aggressive behaviour during the breeding season. Golfers, in particular, seem to arouse odium in the birds. It is wise during such periods to guard the eyes and head, perhaps by wearing a hat and sunglasses.

It is even better, of course, to make friends of the birds by feeding them during the whole year. When the breeding season comes around they will forbear to attack you.

It is true that the clearing of eucalypt woodland has deprived magpies of many of their nesting places. On balance, however, they are one of the few species which is not threatened by the advance of human settlement. In fact, the clearing of forests for the growing of crops has provided them with more food. The one hazard of civilization to which magpies have not adapted is the motor car.

Michelet wrote 'without birds the world would be at the mercy of insects'. Magpies are one of the bird species which help to keep the insect problem under control. In particular, they reduce the impact of locust infestations very efficiently by feeding extensively on the flightless nymphs. Many other insects find their way into the magpie's beak; thus they do the farmer and gardener a great service.

# Currawongs

The name of this bird derives from the cries of 'curra-wa', 'chilla-wong', 'curra-wong', made by the pied currawong, *Strepera graculina*. Most people in Queensland and New South Wales are familiar with the curras, which range all along the coast of eastern Australia, spending spring and winter in the high country and descending to the plains in winter.

Flocks of them even invade cities and suburbs; certain birds often select a particular garden as their domain. They are not likeable birds but they are attention-rivetting, and bemused householders often feed them pieces of meat, repelled but fascinated by the greed with which the birds snatch the pieces of food. Some people even look forward to the appearance in their garden of a particularly greedy and aggressive bird.

Currawongs are sturdily built and grow to about 45cm. They sport black plumage marked with white; their bill is slightly hooked and their eyes are yellow. The two sexes look alike.

They breed in the period from September to March, nesting in the forks of trees, and usually produce three to four eggs. During this period they can be seen breeding in suburbia as well as escaping the hustle and bustle and building their nests in the solitude of the forests of the Great Dividing Range.

Ornithologists describe currawongs as 'birds of the open forest'. They are referring to both the pied currawong and also a second species, the grey currawong, *Strepera versicolor*, which ranges along the southern coast of Australia and throughout Tasmania. This is slightly larger than the pied currawong, growing to about 50cm.

The sounds produced by this species are not uniform throughout its range. The famous British ornithologist John Gould (1804–81) likened them to the musical 'klink, klank, kew' of a blacksmith's anvil. Hence their alternative name of bell magpie. In Western Australia the same species is known as 'the squeaker'.

Currawongs are omnivorous, preying particularly on stick insects and favouring females when their abdomens are distended by eggs. They also enjoy fruit, a taste which makes them very unpopular with orchardists. In Queensland the pied currawong was suspected of spreading prickly pear and extermination campaigns were attempted.

# Whipbirds

When the first settlers heard whips cracking in the bush, they may well have thought that they had been preceded in this country by a band of drovers or stockmen, such is the resemblance of the whipbird's call to a cracking whip. The mystery probably deepened for the bewildered aliens when they were unable to trace the source of the sound, for the whipbird is a shy creature, loathe to present itself to searchers.

Whipbirds are confined to Australia, and even here there are only two species: the eastern whipbird, *Psophodes olivaceus*, and the western whipbird, *P. nigrogularis*. Both are from 24–27 centimetres long, with a broad tail which is approximately half as long as the body. On the head is a small jaunty crest.

The eastern whipbird is dark olive-green on the back and tail, black on the head, crest and beak, and with a large white patch on the side of the throat. The western species is similar in colour to its eastern relative, except for its grey crest and a narrow white stripe on the side of the black throat.

The eastern species with its piercing call soon brought itself to the attention of the early settlers. Being used to the sweet birdsong of English woods, they reacted by giving the bird its common names which included 'coachwhip bird' and 'stockwhip bird'.

Male and female birds 'sing' a duet. The male makes the whipcrack sound, and the female adds 'choo choo'. In *Birds of Australia* (J. D. Macdonald) the eastern bird is described as singing 'happy birthday to you'. The male and female of the western species also 'sing'. Macdonald translates the lyrics as 'its for teacher' by the male and 'pick it up' by the female.

Whipbirds draw attention to themselves only by their call. Otherwise they are unobtrusive almost to the point of invisibility. Their success in achieving virtual invisibility is due not only to their dull colouring, but more particularly to their choice of habitat — the densest, most impenetrable scrub and, in the east, dark temperate rainforest.

They are not strong fliers and are rarely seen in the air. Being insect-eaters, they forage for food on the ground, turning over vegetative litter with their powerful feet. Their tails often have a worn look which is most likely due to abrasion from the dense vegetation.

Mating is no brief encounter for the whipbirds: when a bond is formed between male and female it endures. The prospective parents build a cup-shaped nest from twigs and grass, and site it so as to discourage intruders, such as in a high clump of prickly bushes. Only the female incubates the eggs, which are bluish, spotted with black. The eggs hatch in ten to twelve days and, when the young emerge, they are fed by their parents until they can take care of themselves.

The great English ornithologist, John Gould, described the western species from a single specimen collected by the explorer, John Gilbert, near Perth in 1842. For the next hundred years or so it was believed that this species had become extinct. However, it is now known to inhabit isolated country on Kangaroo Island, on the Eyre and Yorke Peninsulas of South Australia, and in the Victorian mallee.

The eastern species occupies areas of rain forest along the east coast from southern Queensland to southern Victoria and also in the area behind Mackay and on the Atherton Table-land.

E. & D. Hosking/NPIAW

The western whipbirds are threatened by extensive clearing of scrub and forest and subsequent land development, in South Australia, Western Australia and the eastern States.

Ornithologists believe that populations will continue to survive in nature reserves, such as those at Two People's Bay, Western Australia, Flinders Island, and at Innes at the southern tip of the Yorke Peninsula.

---

*TOP: The small jaunty crest on this eastern whipbird's head makes it appear as if it has just been woken up and hasn't had a chance to fix its feathers in place.*
*BELOW: It's their call which draws attention and certainly not their appearance as highlighted by this western whipbird which easily blends into its surroundings. This is one of Australia's rarest birds.*

The establishment of a national park at Innes was, in fact, prompted by the finding of the birds in the area.

However, even in these sanctuaries some of which are quite small, the species could be destroyed by bushfires which often sweep parks and reserves.

# Bellbirds

The call of the bellbird is one of the most pleasant and unmistakable sounds of southeastern forests. These calls which carry a great distance, help the birds which live in colonies, to locate other members of their group.

The bellbird, a more popular name for the bell miner, *Manorina melanophrys* is a member of an endemic group of miner bird which inhabit the edge of wet schlerophyll forests and thick

CSIRO L. A. Moore/NPIAW

woodland areas near water from the southern Queensland coast southward to Melbourne.

They are sometimes seen in city suburbs in Victoria but are never found west of the Great Dividing Range. Drivers travelling the old Pacific Highway between Newcastle and Sydney are often entertained by the bellbirds along the wooded areas of the road near Gosford and the central coast.

## Long-lease residents

Dense colonies of bell miners often stay in the same place for many years and keep other species from invading their territories. They are more tightly packed than their close relative, the noisy miner which is known to congregate in groups of 8 to 10 birds to the hectare.

In some bell miner colonies in southern Queensland when taller trees have died, a breakdown of colonies has followed. There have also been reports of hundreds of bell miners suddenly leaving an area. This could have occurred due to food shortages. Bell miners are honeyeaters and feed at flowering trees although their principal food consists of insects especially lerps.

The bellbird is an active, gregarious bird which stands 18 centimetres tall. Both sexes have a similar appearance.

*ABOVE: Bellbirds or bell miners live in colonies and it is through their call that they can locate members of the colony. Feeding the young is a community affair, with bellbirds often queuing up to feed the fledglings.*

The head, back and rump are olive green with the darkest section on the crown. There is a patch of orange-red, naked skin behind the eye, contrasting with the dark brown eye. The underparts are light, yellow-green, the wings and tail are brown and the bill and legs are bright orange-yellow.

Only the female bird builds the nest but several birds will visit a nest to feed the young and often queue up to wait their turn. Even after the young

*LEFT: Bellbirds' ideal habitat: a densely wooded forest somewhere along the southeastern coast of Australia. Colonies of bellbirds will remain in the one region for years, strongly defending their territories from invasion by other species.*

birds leave the nest they are fed by a number of birds and remain close together for several days.

A single brood will be fed by older birds an average of 46 times an hour during the first 14 days of their life. When 30 days old the young fledglings can fend for themselves.

Bellbirds usually breed from July to February but also in the period from April to June. Their nests are loosely-woven cups of thin twigs, grasses and shredded bark, lightly lined with root-lets and downy seeds.

Nests are usually suspended from tree forks, sometimes close to the ground but usually four to five metres up in a sapling or tree. They are bound to supporting branches with cobwebs, moss, lichen, leaves, insect egg cases or cocoons.

The bellbird usually lays two eggs but has been known to lay just a single egg or as many as three. They are pale pink spotted with chestnut, red or purple-brown colourings. Incubation time is 15 days.

Bellbirds have a special trick to distract intruders away from their nests. The bird first waves its wings and calls harshly. Then it drops suddenly to the ground and repeats the performance in the undergrowth. The theatrics are well-staged and seem to work.

# Butcherbirds

From its perch high on a television antenna or on a tree in a suburban park, the tuneful tones of the butcher-bird can often be heard on the still, morning air. The voice of this well-known songster producing pure tonal notes is one of the most pleasing sounds to the human ear.

Butcherbirds belong to one of the best known families of Australian birds which includes magpies and curra-wongs. Members of this genus have the habit of preying upon animals which are too large to be swallowed whole. Their diet includes large insects especially grasshoppers and small animals which have to be torn up.

They manage this tearing process by means of a sharp, black hook at the tip of a large bill. The captured food is held down by the feet or wedged in a sharp-angled notch or stuck fast on a spike. These birds are mostly arboreal but often hop along the ground on their short legs. They feed off the ground but will also carry food into trees to be eaten.

## The pied butcherbird

The black-throated or pied butcher-bird is widespread throughout the country except in the extreme south of the continent and the tip of Cape York Peninsula. It frequents open wood-land, scrubland and suburban parks and is probably most abundant in the partly cleared pastoral country of the inland.

Noted for its fine singing which has been described as loud, flute-like notes, the pied butcherbird often engages in duets with a mate in which each bird sings alternately. One of its favourite singing perches is a tall, dead tree from which its musical renditions often travel a great distance.

Pied butcherbirds live mostly in family groups, with up to six birds in the one gathering. This group appears to occupy much of the same territory year after year. Juveniles are a rather plain brown and probably do not gain their full pied plumage until they are about 18 months old. These young birds remain with their parents and sometimes help with raising their young siblings.

113

# The black butcherbird

The secretive black butcherbird lurks among vegetation in mangroves, monsoonal forests and rainforest scrub of northern Australia. It is confined to a small coastal strip from New Guinea and Cape York down the Queensland coast and is common in the Cooktown to Tully region. It can also be found along a small coastal strip at the top of the Northern Territory.

The black butcherbird is heard more often than it is seen. Its very musical voice has been described as a rich yodelling call and like the pied butcherbird it takes part in duets with each bird contributing part of the complete song.

Standing about 36 centimetres tall, the black butcherbird has entirely black plumage and its bill is a pale blue-grey with a black tip. These birds are sedentary and are usually seen in pairs although they have been observed in small groups usually after the breeding season.

The black butcherbird feeds on a varied diet of small birds and their eggs, insects, crustaceans, reptiles, frogs and fruit. It builds a bowl-shaped nest of sticks and twigs in the fork of a tree.

These nests are usually built 10 metres above the ground in tall eucalypts or paperbark trees or about two metres above the ground in mangrove locations. Between two and four olive green eggs are laid and breeding time is between September and February.

## The black-backed butcherbird

Usually seen in pairs, the black-backed butcherbird of Cape York Peninsula is a particularly friendly bird and is often a regular visitor to established camps

*T. & P. Gardner/A.N.T. Photo Library*

---

*OPPOSITE TOP: These young pied butcherbirds which are being fed by their parents will probably not gain their full pied plumage until they are 18 months old. Until then they will remain a rather drab brown and white colour.*
*LEFT: The black butcherbird is heard more often than it is seen. It inhabits the rainforests and mangrove areas of northern and northeastern Australia.*

and houses at the top end of Cape York.

The voices of these birds are softer and not quite as musical as other butcherbirds although their whistling which is often sung alternately by male and female is always appreciated.

## The grey butcherbird

Rated with hawks as a terror to small birds, the grey butcherbird has the habit of diving down from its perch and seizing its prey on the ground. It then tears it apart in the same manner as a hawk or crow.

Grey butcherbirds prefer heavily wooded country and can be found over much of the wooded parts of the continent excluding the desert regions and Cape York Peninsula. They choose a permanent territory in which to live and nest in the same place year after year.

*ABOVE: Grey butcherbirds also have a beautiful call; only their voices are lower in pitch than for those of the other butcherbirds. The whole group is known as being excellent songsters.*

---

They feed on insects, lizards, mice and a few fruits and seeds. Near suburban homes or in built-up areas, grey butcherbirds will often accept offerings of meat.

The grey butcherbird is also noted for its beautiful voice. Like other butcherbirds, this species often sings duets with a mate in which each bird sings alternately.

Their voices are distinctly different from the other butcherbirds: the tone is slightly harsher and the pitch is lower. A grey butcherbird will often send forth a burst of loud, rollicking phrases and also mimic other birds.

Parent grey butcherbirds will fiercely defend their nests and attack any intruder with a snapping action of their sharp, hooked bills.

# FASCINATING FINCHES

*Introduced and indigenous, finches live in a variety of different habitats throughout Australia. They are also a very popular species for aviaries. However, successful captivity of these birds usually means dedicated aviculturalists recreating the finches' natural environment.*

Australian finches have become very popular as cage birds: they are beautiful, have a sociable nature, fascinating behaviour pattern and are easy to breed and feed. They share world popularity with the canary and the parrot as a pet bird.

At large, finches usually inhabit the grasslands. Australia has about 18 kinds of native finches, related to almost 100 other species found in Asia and Africa, grouped in the family of weaver finches, small seed-eating birds.

A German naturalist, Dr K Immelmann, is accepted as a world authority on finches. His *Australian Finches* is a definitive reference work for these birds, describing and analysing their habits and lifestyles.

Finches hop along the ground, taking off with both feet simultaneously, searching for seed, their main food. However, during the breeding period most birds also catch insects, in the air or on the ground. The mating swarm of termites, filling the sky, is like a gigantic smorgasbord for finches which eat a path through the excited termites. Finches are fast flyers and can cover long distances.

Some finches have unusual drinking styles. A few species, such as the zebra finch, suck water directly, like pigeons — uncommon among perching birds. Most birds fill the bill with

*TOP: A pair of zebra finches, the female (left) and male. When drinking water, these finches like some of the other Australian finches have the ability to suck up water directly rather than sipping and then tilting the head back. Zebra finches are popular cage birds.*

*RIGHT: The painted firetail (this one is male) has the more common habit of sipping its drinking water then raising its head to swallow.*

R. & D. Keller/A.N.T. Photo Library

water, then tilt up the head enabling the water to run down through their throat.

Most of the finches, being social birds, gather in large flocks. During the breeding season, a pair will leave the flock for a few hours each day and search for a nesting site, in a small tree or in a bush.

The female is the dominant partner of a couple which seem to pair for life. Nesting is a laborious process, started by the male who goes out to find a suitable spot, then calls the female to inspect it. Scientists record that males may propose over a hundred nesting sites before the fussy female relents and accepts one.

Finches lay several eggs and most species begin incubation when the fourth egg has been laid. In some hot

parts of Australia, incubation stops when the temperature soars to 37°C. In the southern states, winter is too cold for nesting even though food may be available, and so breeding takes place in the spring.

# Major Finch Species

The most notable Australian species:

The zebra finch, *Poephila guttata*, found in most parts of the Australian mainland has an amazing ability to withstand very high concentrations of salt in its drinking water. It likes woodlands, open and dry country but

*ABOVE: The most trusting of all the firetails, red-browed firetails are a very sociable bird, in many instances remaining in groups both during and outside the breeding season.*

not the forests. It builds a dome-shaped nest and is known for its nasal voice.

The blue-faced finch, *Erythrura trichroa*, is a recent arrival from islands to the north of Australia. It has a clear preference for the tropical north around Cape York where edges of mangroves and rainforests provide its shelter. Little is known about its habits and breeding patterns as this finch keeps mainly to bushes and low trees and is solitary or moves around in small flocks.

The Gouldian finch, *Chloebia gouldiae*, named by pioneer scientist John Gould after his wife, is perhaps the most spectacular and beautiful though not the best known of Australian finches. It's found in tropical Australia, seldom far from water and prefers a habitat of grassy areas.

The star finch, *Neochmia ruficauda*, lives around grassy borders of inland water and feeds on flying termites and ants while clinging to grass stems and twigs. This is one species which drinks by sucking; the male carries a grass stem in his bill during a courtship display.

---

*BELOW: Although not very common, the beautiful firetail can be found along the coastline stretching from Sydney to Adelaide, including Tasmania. Wilson's Promontory is the only exception to this. However on various offshore islands along this particular stretch of coastline and in Tasmania, the beautiful firetail is much more common and more trusting. These are the areas where the beautiful firetail's habitat has not been as adversely affected by the influence of humans.*

The spice finch, *Lonchura punctulata*, which was introduced, is a common species which often thrives at the expense of other finches. It lives in the bushy savannas, has flexible feeding habits and breeds in most months, laying six to seven white eggs.

# The Firetails

Firetails are easily recognised by the brilliant red blaze across their rumps, which may extend for a short distance along the body. They also have characteristic red beaks and eye markings.

The scientific name for the five species of firetail is *Emblema*, a Greek word that means 'tessellated pavement'. Originally this was only applied to the painted firetail, *E. pictum*, the other firetails being classified in this genus some years later.

No doubt the idea of a tessellated pavement came from white spots on the side and breast of the painted firetail, which are quite distinctive on their black background. The other firetails, except for the red-browed, also share similar markings, either in

the form of spots or stripes.

Courtship among the firetails is highly ritualised, and intriguing to watch. Although the actions vary between species, all involve the holding of grass stems, which possibly signifies the nest-building drive within the bird. Some firetails bob up and down exaggeratedly, such as in the red-eared firetail, where the male jumps between two branches before bobbing up and down on the spot.

All the firetails are small birds, ranging in size from 10 to 12 centimetres in length. In habitat they vary a great deal. Three are found in dense coastal scrub, while the other two are birds of the dry inland; one of the latter two, the painted firetail, is the only finch to have successfully penetrated the arid zone.

## The painted firetail

Because of its dry environment, the painted firetail is quite different in many ways from the other firetails. It is primarily a ground dwelling bird, very much at home on spinifex plains and rocky gorges from Central Queensland to the Western Australian

Pep S Photo/NPIAW

*ABOVE: The rare, shy red-eared firetail has suffered more than any other finch under the influence of humans. Its characteristic markings are red patches on the rump and tail, a red ear patch and spotted sides.*

coast. In some towns, such as Alice Springs, it has been observed in gardens in small flocks.

Distribution tends to be patchy, since the painted firetail is dependant on small permanent waterholes. It is a sedentary bird, rarely seen in large numbers, but moving about in loose groups. Unlike the other firetails it is not highly sociable, contact between individuals being kept to a minimum.

They can usually be observed hopping over the sandy soil between tussocks of spinifex grass, searching for grass seeds. Rarely will they take seeds directly from the plant stem. The painted firetails' mode of drinking is unusual among dry country birds. Instead of drinking in the sucking

fashion, like pigeons, they take single sips and tilt their head back to swallow.

With the shortage of tall trees and shrubs in the centre, painted firetails have adapted their nesting habits accordingly. The nest is built in a clump of spinifex, about 30–60 centimetres above the ground. A platform of twigs, stones and earth is constructed first, followed by a flimsy, globular nest composed of almost any vegetation the birds can find.

Four white eggs are usually laid, with incubation governed by the daily temperatures; in hot weather there may be no need for the birds to stay with the eggs during the day. The young hatch after about 12 days and are fledged at three weeks of age.

## The red-browed firetail

East coast dwellers will almost certainly be familiar with the red-browed

firetail, also known simply as the redhead, *E. temporalis*. Their colouring is such that they may not be noticed until the observer is within a few metres. When disturbed, the flock of 10–20 birds takes flight immediately, uttering a high-pitched 'ssee ssee' call.

The red-browed firetail lacks the usual spots or stripes found in the other firetails, and the red rump is duller than in most. However, this is compensated by the bright red band extending from the beak across the head. This band is longer in the female and also more tapered.

Red-browed firetails can be found along the entire length of the east coast and across to Adelaide. There is also a small population near Perth, established by aviary escapees. They are common in many parks and gardens and are the most trusting of firetails.

These are highly sociable birds and remain in a group throughout the year. Pairs apparently mate for life and are never far apart. Outside of the breeding season several birds may group together in a roosting nest for added warmth.

The red-browed feeds on a wide variety of seeding grasses, herbs and soft berries. Insects are also taken, usually gleaned from the foliage of shrubs. They rarely take insects 'on the wing' as is common with many other finches.

Like other firetails, except the painted firetail, the red-browed builds a bottle-shaped nest, with an extended entrance opening. This is placed in any dense bush, about two metres above the ground. Thorny bushes are preferred, including the introduced blackberry and rose bushes.

## The beautiful firetail

The beautiful firetail, *E. bellum*, is considerably more restricted in range than the red-browed. It is confined to the coast from Sydney to Adelaide, Tasmania and various offshore islands. It's not common anywhere on the mainland except at Wilsons Promontory. In Tasmania and on the islands it is still fairly common, and more trusting than on the mainland.

Extensive clearing of coastal land has seriously depleted the habitat of the beautiful firetail. Thick belts of tea-tree scrub, interspersed by casuarina stands, are preferred. The vegetation is normally very thick, making observation difficult.

In habits the beautiful firetail is very much like the red-browed, and is often seen feeding in company with this species. It is, however, more closely allied to the red-eared firetail of Western Australia, *E. oculatum*.

## The red-eared firetail

The red-eared firetail is a rare, shy bird, confined to dense heathlands in the south-west corner of Western Australia.

It has suffered more than any other finch from European settlement. In appearance it is similar to the beautiful firetail, but is spotted along the side, and has a short red brow behind the eyes.

Unlike the beautiful firetail, it does not form flocks outside the breeding season, but remains in pairs in loosely defined territories throughout the year.

This territory extends from 100–200 metres across, but only the vicinity of the nest is strongly defended.

## The diamond firetail

The final member of the firetails is the diamond firetail, *E. guttatum*. It is found in open grasslands with scattered stands of trees and scrub throughout south-eastern Australia.

They are highly sociable birds, often seen hopping across the ground in search of ripe and half-ripe grass seeds and small insects. Feeding seems to be almost totally restricted to the ground, to the same extent as in the painted firetail.

The diamond firetail, in accordance with its dry habitat, does not sip as the other firetails do when drinking, but sucks the water up in long bursts. This allows it to exploit the smallest pool of water, but does leave it vulnerable to predators, since the eyes are directed downwards for a relatively long period.

The diamond firetail performs the most elaborate courtship display of all the firetails. The male takes a length of grass, up to one metre long, in his beak and flies up to the further-most branches of a tree. The female follows him and watches the first part of his dance passively. The male stretches his neck downwards and fluffs up his feathers, then starts bobbing up and down. During this phase he utters a rasping song.

The female approaches the male and as she draws close he twists and

*ABOVE: The beautiful little diamond firetail is also known as the diamond sparrow. This firetail also drinks by sucking up the water.*

lowers his head, offering his opened beak. This is highly suggestive of a begging youngster and is common in many birds. Soon after this the female flies to the nest site and quivers her tail, thus inviting copulation.

# Firetails in the aviary

Firetails are extremely popular with aviculturists, but results in captivity are usually mixed. Only the diamond firetail and the painted firetail can be said to have adapted to captivity. Here they will breed quite freely given the right conditions. The red-browed firetail is often kept in aviaries, but does not settle down to aviary life well. In contrast to its habits in the wild, it is shy and retiring in captivity.

The red-eared and beautiful firetails are rarely seen in aviaries, and almost never appear on the open market for sale. No doubt there is a small but profitable black market operation, as they are highly prized, both in Australia and overseas.

Those that have been kept in captivity usually do not live long; the only successes have come from truly dedicated aviculturists who are prepared to recreate the birds' natural environment, on a large scale.

In the case of both these birds it is

*LEFT: The blue-faced finch is found around tropical Cape York.*
*BOTTOM LEFT: Another inhabitant of tropical Australia, the Gouldian finch is so known following pioneer ornithologist John Gould naming this bird after his wife.*
*BOTTOM RIGHT: Star finches are found in dense grass areas surrounding inland waterways.*

important to establish captive breeding stocks to ensure their survival.

The most important criterion in breeding firetails is to provide an aviary that reproduces the birds' natural environment. In the case of the painted firetail, this would mean a sandy enclosure, planted with spinifex, with a few large rocks for the birds to perch on. In contrast to this the red-browed firetail requires a heavily planted aviary.

In all cases a large aviary is a must: at least two metres high, two metres wide, and five metres in length, with a shelter at one end. Only the diamond firetail will tolerate a smaller aviary. If you can't come up with the goods, then leave the firetails to the experts.

# BIRDS OF THE NIGHT

*As night begins to fall a change of guard takes place in Australia's forests. As the daytime birds retire to their roosts the nocturnal ones prepare for a night's hunting. Most suited to this environment is the owl, a wonderful example of natural selection and adaptation.*

## Hawk Owls and Barn Owls

Few predators have attained such a high level of anatomical sophistication as the owl, enabling it to fill and control its ecological niche with little threat to its dominance.

The owl's feathers are particularly soft, and they extend right down to the talons. This gives the owl excellent soundproofing, enabling it to swoop on its prey with little or no noise. The colour of the feathers, soft browns and whites, gives it camouflage when resting during the day.

The feet are well adapted for seizing and gripping, as in most birds of prey, but with one further refinement. The outer toe is able to move sideways, giving the foot a bigger spread to compensate for any inaccuracy when striking.

As a further aid to night hunting, owls have developed remarkable vision. The eyes are large and, though owls cannot see in total darkness, they operate efficiently with a minimum of light from the moon and stars.

*LEFT: Although not seen very often, the boobook owl is the most common member of the owl family. Boobooks often reside in suburban areas. These two boobooks are juveniles.*
*BELOW: The smallest and most abundant of the owls is the southern boobook owl.*

Owls also possess binocular vision, similar to humans. This means that they cannot see to the side, but can judge distances extremely well. To look sideways owls must turn their heads, giving rise to the myth that owls can turn their heads 360°. That they cannot.

Despite their excellent night vision, owls rely to a great extent on their superior hearing to locate their prey. Unlike most animals, their ears are not symmetrically placed. Sounds reach their ears at different angles, allowing the owl to quickly locate its next meal. These adaptations make the owl one of the most efficient hunters in the world.

Australia has only eight of the world's 136 species of owl, but they have colonised almost every area of the continent. The Australian owls are divided into two families, the hawk owls, Strigidae, and the barn owls, Tytonidae.

Bay Picture Library

I. R. McCann/A.N.T. Photo Library

*LEFT: A member of the barn owl family, the masked owl can kill animals as large as rabbits. The Tasmanian subspecies of the barn owl is one of the largest members of the barn owl family in the world.*

*BELOW LEFT: Rarest of Australian owls is the grass owl which lives in eastern coastal grassland areas. Small tunnels in the grass are often the only indication of the grass owl's existence in a region.*

*ABOVE: Barn owl numbers fluctuate widely. If there is a mice plague, numbers will jump and if food is scarce, barn owls will rapidly decline.*

## The boobook

The most common member of the first family is the boobook owl, found in all areas of Australia, and also in New Zealand, New Guinea and some Indonesian islands. The boobook has taken up residence in many suburban areas, but it is not often seen: like most other owls, it is rather shy. The only indication of its presence is the characteristic cuckoo-like call — boo-book — from which it takes its name.

The chief foods of the boobook are mice, small birds and a very high proportion of insects. In suburban areas sparrows are particularly favoured, as are the multitude of insects that gather around street lights.

# The powerful owl

Less common than the boobook is the powerful owl, a veritable giant among owls. It reaches a length of about 60 centimetres, twice the size of the boobook. The powerful owl inhabits the wet sclerophyll forests along the east coast from Rockhampton in Queensland, to Portland in Victoria.

As its size indicates, it is not restricted to feeding on sparrows and mice. It prefers gliders — eating these almost exclusively in some areas — small possums, rats and mice and birds such as magpies and kookaburras.

Powerful owls are strongly territorial and will defend their area against any members of the same species. They develop a good knowledge of this area and they glide amongst the trees and gullies with remarkable speed.

Generally the call of the powerful owl is enough to deter intruders. The famous early naturalist John Gould described it as a 'hoarse loud mournful note', resembling the sound of a 'bleating ox'.

# The barking and rufous owl

Perhaps the most misunderstood of our owls is the barking owl. Early settlers camped in the bush at night sometimes heard a high-pitched scream that resembled the cry of a woman in extreme terror. Investigation found that the barking owl was responsible and it quickly earned the bush name of 'screaming woman bird'.

The more common call of the barking owl resembles a dog or fox barking, with an occasional growl thrown in for good measure. It is fairly common in open woodland, where it feeds on rabbits, young hares, rats and mice, making it a favourite with graziers.

Small marsupials and birds are also included in the diet, but the prevalence of the introduced pests makes them almost standard fare for the barking owl.

The only other Australian member of the hawk owl family is the rufous owl. An inhabitant of the rainforests of the far north, where it feeds on small tree-dwelling mammals, it has been studied little due to its shy nature.

H. & J. Beste/Auscape Int.

# The barn owl

Like the hawk owls, the other family of Australian owls, the barn owls, cover a wide range of terrains. The namesake of the group, the barn owl, *Tyto alba*, is the most widespread, covering all areas except western Tasmania.

Their numbers fluctuate widely in relation to the food supply: a plague of mice will see a dramatic rise in the barn owl population, with an equally dramatic fall after the plague.

Like the other members of this family, the barn owl is not too fussy about where it roosts and nests. If no suitable trees are available, it will use a cave, a shed, or even a well. In fact, anywhere which is private and offers enough room for raising a family of up to six chicks.

# The masked owl

The masked owl is another member of the barn owl family. It occurs throughout Australia, except in the dry centre,

*ABOVE: The Papuan frogmouth has a blend of mottled grey, brown and buff plumage which enables it to easily match its surroundings. Frogmouths are nocturnal and eat frogs, mice, insects and lizards.*

but is not particularly numerous. In habits it is similar to the barn owl, but it will take larger game. The Tasmanian subspecies of masked owl is the largest member of the barn owl family in the world, and commonly feeds on mammals up to the size of rabbits.

# The sooty and the grass owls

Little has been written about the last two owls in this family, the sooty owl and grass owl. The former inhabits thick forests along the east coast, roosting amongst dense vegetation and in caves.

The grass owl is the rarest of our owls. It is a ground dweller, primarily found in grasslands in eastern coastal areas, with rare but regular sightings further inland. Often the only indications of its presence are the small tunnels it makes through the grass. Extensive research is needed to establish its range and status and to ensure its survival.

# Frogmouths

Like owls, the frogmouths are nocturnal and well camouflaged by their cryptic plumage. They also bear the same soft feathers for silent flight and huge eyes specially adapted for night vision. However their small weak feet and huge gaping mouths distinguish them from owls, which they superficially resemble.

The frogmouths are aptly named; their wide flat bill and enormous gape give them an unusual, some think grotesque, appearance. Their plumage is a soft blend of mottled greys, browns and buffs which is perfectly matched to their surroundings and so varies in different parts of Australia.

They are masters of camouflage, not only in colour but also in behaviour. During the day they are inactive and roost close to the trunk of rough-barked trees or on dead wood. When approached they gradually elongate and stiffen their bodies at a 35–45° angle to the branch and jut their head skywards, taking on the appearance of a grey, weatherbeaten broken-off branch. Even when pointed out, they are difficult to see as they sit motionless, watching the intruder through eyes narrowed to slits.

At dusk frogmouths are more easily disturbed and stare with wide golden eyes before flushing. They fly slowly and, not being adapted for sustained flight, only travel a short distance. They prefer woodland and hunt from

C. Webster/A.N.T. Photo Library

Jean-Paul Ferrero/Auscape Int.

a tree or fence post, using a perch and pounce strategy. Other members of the order catch mainly flying insects but frogmouths feed mainly on animals and insects snatched from the ground.

## The Papuan frogmouth

The largest of the frogmouths is the Papuan frogmouth, which, as its name suggests, is centred in Papua New Guinea, but is also found in north-eastern Australia in rainforests and thickly wooded country on Cape York. It frequents forest clearings, often roosting in pairs or groups by day and at dusk beginning to search the trees and ground for insects, frogs, lizards and mice. Like the other frogmouths, it builds a flimsy platform of twigs on

a branch or fork, sometimes lined with green leaves, and sits lengthwise and low to the branch when incubating.

## The marbled frogmouth

Marbled frogmouths look like a small Papuan frogmouth, but have a more conspicuously tufted group of feathers above their nostrils than the other two frogmouths which is thought to help snare insects. Like the other two frogmouths, they eat on the ground as

well as insects found on the bases of trunk, branches and leaves of trees. They are restricted to rainforest and are seldom seen in Australia, particularly in recent times. Their decline in numbers has come as a result of clearing of lowland rainforest. It is now an endangered bird.

## The tawny frogmouth

The tawny frogmouth is the most numerous and widespread of the three frogmouths, found wherever there are trees with the exception of rainforest.

---

*BELOW: Blending beautifully with its background, the large-tailed nightjar is the perfect example of perfect camouflage. This nightjar is sedentary, living in humid rainforest and dense monsoon scrub year round.*

It is more grey than tawny in colour and looks very pale at night, when it is most often seen. Members of family groups will roost together, side by side, sometimes on the ground or on fallen timber.

At twilight they separate and look for food like moths, mantids, cockroaches, ants, snails, reptiles, birds and mice, battering mice against the ground before swallowing them whole. They will hunt from roadside posts, picking up animals crossing the road and insects attracted to lights, and, as

a result, are quite often hit by cars. Their call is a soft ooo or oom, although at one time they were thought to make the often heard 'mopoke' call now known to belong to the boobook owl.

# Nightjars

The nightjars are migratory; their dependence on flying insects for food means that they must move to survive. They are the nocturnal equivalents of swifts and swallows, catching insects on the wing. Flying open-mouthed through the air 'trawling' for insects, their jaws snap shut when prey hits the roof of their mouth. They spend much of their time on the wing and usually crouch when perched, so, having little need for them, their feet are almost rudimentary.

The nightjars are all vulnerable, particularly when nesting, to predation or trampling by cats, foxes, dogs, and livestock. The tawny frogmouth and Papuan frogmouth have benefited from the greater feeding opportunities offered in partially cleared land. On the other hand, white-throated nightjars are probably adversely affected by clearing of areas where they nest on the forest floor. Nightjars, like the frogmouths, have cryptic plumage which merges perfectly with the ground soil and litter on which they nest. Their eggs are also cryptically coloured, unlike the white eggs of the frogmouths. Similarly, their chicks are almost impossible to see in their leaf-litter nest. Only their eyes give away their position and like the frogmouths they keep them shut when threatened.

The nightjars' mottled tones are interrupted by white areas on the throat, wings and tail which are hidden at the nest but flashed during aerial courtship and territorial displays. Their flight is characteristically jerky, twisting and silent. Only their persistent calling, usually while breeding, belies their presence. They have peculiar calls that pierce the night air and give them their name. There are three nightjars in Australia. They are found in more or less separate areas and between them are distributed over the whole of the mainland. The one owlet nightjar is ubiquitous.

their egg is also a problem on the sun-baked rocks of Central Australia. The related nighthawk of North America is able to keep its eggs at 46°C by shading them, with spread wings, while the surface on which it nests soars to 61°C.

## The large-tailed nightjar

The large-tailed nightjar is found in the tropical coastal north and north-east, preferring wetter areas than the spotted nightjar. Its call is a familiar sound of tropical nights, a loud repeated chop, like the sound of an axe hitting a hollow log, thus its local name, the axe-bird. Unlike most nightjars it is sedentary, living in humid rainforest and dense monsoon scrub all year. It frequents the edges of forest and of clearings, needing the open space for hunting and the cover for nesting and roosting. Its food is like that of the other nightjars — mantids, flying ants, moths, cicadas and other winged insects.

## The owlet nightjar

The smallest of Australia's nightbirds, little bigger than a starling, the owlet nightjar is also the most widespread. It is most numerous in the arid zone, roosting by day in tree hollows or holes in cliff faces. It does not assume the broken branch attitude of the frogmouths probably because it roosts in enclosed places, but does have similar plumage. With a small beak, enormous brown eyes and black striped head it has an engaging owl-like appearance.

Small birds often mob owlet nightjars, presumably because of this resemblance to owls as the nightjars are certainly no threat to them. Facial bristles, projecting beyond its beak help it sense its world. Once a year they lay three or four eggs in a hollow. They combine the perch and pounce hunting method of the frogmouths, with the swifter chase of flying insects used by the true nightjars.

Owlet nightjars are disadvantaged when the trees, with the hollows on which they are dependent, are cut down or fall down and are not replaced by younger trees. Starlings and other introduced species place greater pressure on them by also competing for hollows.

## The white-throated nightjar

The white-throated nightjar makes a loud, laughing call as it flies. Its eye, caught by car headlights, is a brilliant red. Found down the entire east coast, it is seldom seen. It migrates in loose flocks of as many as twenty birds which hawk for insects flushed from the treetops. The more southern birds move the greatest distance, leapfrogging the more sedentary northern birds to winter in New Guinea. Each spring they return to the same territory to nest on ridges in dry open forest.

## Spotted nightjars

Spotted nightjars do not overlap greatly the range of the white-throated nightjar and are patchily distributed across the rest of Australia. In some areas they are quite common and are most often seen when their ruby red

*ABOVE: Owlet nightjars live in tree hollows or holes in cliff faces. This is the smallest of Australia's nightbirds, and is also the most widespread.*

eyes and white wing spots are illuminated by car lights. They are most numerous in the stony ridges and ranges of Central Australia, laying their single egg amongst the rocks. Like the other nightjars they will perform a distraction display when disturbed at their nest by flapping and stumbling about. Their chick leaves the nest scrape soon after hatching and is fed regurgitated wads of insect. When it is about a month old it begins to hawk insects for itself.

Spotted nightjars often roost at sites that are exposed for part of the day to the full force of the sun and can tolerate temperatures in excess of 40°C. How they survive in such extreme temperatures is not fully known but they keep their body temperature under control by panting or using some other means of cooling by evaporative water loss. Overheating of

ISBN 1-86256-037-4

9 781862 560376

T3-APC-906